NEW DIRECTIONS FOR HIGHER EDUCATION

Martin Kramer, *University of California, Ber*
EDITOR-IN-CHIEF

P9-BZL-856

Assessment and Curriculum Reform

James L. Ratcliff
Pennsylvania State University

EDITOR

Number 80, Winter 1992

JOSSEY-BASS PUBLISHERS
San Francisco

ASSESSMENT AND CURRICULUM REFORM
James L. Ratcliff (ed.)
New Directions for Higher Education, no. 80
Martin Kramer, Editor-in-Chief

Microfilm copies of issues and articles are available in 16mm and 35mm, as well as microfiche in 105mm, through University Microfilms Inc., 300 North Zeeb Road, Ann Arbor, Michigan 48106.

LC 85-644752   ISSN 0271-0560   ISBN 1-55542-735-9

NEW DIRECTIONS FOR HIGHER EDUCATION is part of The Jossey-Bass Higher and Adult Education Series and is published quarterly by Jossey-Bass Inc., Publishers, 350 Sansome Street, San Francisco, California 94104-1310 (publication number USPS 990-880). Second-class postage paid at San Francisco, California, and at additional mailing offices. POSTMASTER: Send address changes to New Directions for Higher Education, Jossey-Bass Inc., Publishers, 350 Sansome Street, San Francisco, California 94104-1310.

SUBSCRIPTIONS for 1992 cost $45.00 for individuals and $60.00 for institutions, agencies, and libraries.

EDITORIAL CORRESPONDENCE should be sent to the Editor-in-Chief, Martin Kramer, 2807 Shasta Road, Berkeley, California 94708.

Cover photograph and random dot by Richard Blair/Color & Light © 1990.

 The paper used in this journal is acid-free and meets the strictest guidelines in the United States for recycled paper (50 percent recycled waste, including 10 percent postconsumer waste). Manufactured in the United States of America.

CONTENTS

EDITOR'S NOTES

The primary value to be derived from the assessment of undergraduate student learning is to guide the way to more effective education programs and, ultimately, to improved student performance. For assessments to be of value in improving student learning, they must not simply tell us how well students have learned but also link that learning to students' educational experiences. Assessments of student learning in general education are particularly difficult to marshal in comprehensive research universities, doctorate-granting institutions, and comprehensive colleges. In these types of institutions, the curricula and the programs are diverse, often consisting of thousands of courses loosely organized into distributional plans of general education.

Students who take different coursework learn different content, cognitive skills, values, and attitudes. Student learning varies greatly in complex institutions of higher education because of their broad arrays of curriculum offerings. Critical to the success of a general education for students in these institutions is some means for recognizing curriculum diversity and its effects. Thus, the more complex the curriculum offerings, the greater the challenge to determine the relationship between coursework completed and learning achieved.

This volume, *Assessment and Curriculum Reform,* is about linking assessments of students' learning with the patterns of their coursework. We illustrate how and why assessment and curriculum reform need to be combined, and we describe an innovative way in which to use student transcripts and college catalogues to analyze the curriculum so as to associate the coursework of students with the learning that they gain. We therein also show how such assessment data can be used to examine questions about the curriculum, faculty development, and student advising.

In Chapter One, I examine the issues shaping our capacity and need to determine which parts of the college curriculum contribute to improvement in the general learned abilities of undergraduates. The Coursework Cluster Analysis Model (CCAM), a method for linking the patterns of courses in which students enroll with the specific learning that they evidence on assessments, is described. The CCAM was developed through an innovative empirical approach to determine the effects of different patterns of coursework on the general learned abilities of students. This model has proved valid and reliable across a variety of higher education institutions and student populations.

In Chapter Two, Marilyn J. Amey describes how college catalogues have been used in conjunction with the CCAM to determine the extent of change occurring within a diverse curriculum. College catalogues were

examined for several years at four institutions. Some academic departments evidenced an increase in the number of curriculum additions, while
other departments were relatively stable across time. As Amey demonstrates, by examining the nature, scope, and structure of the curriculum, we
can identify constraints on students' course-taking behavior.

In the past few years, there have been many debates regarding the
desirability and effectiveness of the core curriculum as a means to increase
student learning. Advocates of a more culturally and ethnically diverse
curriculum debate the advantages of required and elective diversity courses.
Proponents of critical thinking argue for required, purposeful courses to
accelerate students' abilities in that area. Those concerned with the quality
of undergraduate education and the provision of common learning often
argue for a core curriculum as well. In Chapter Three, Elizabeth A. Jones
provides a way to empirically examine whether a core curriculum is
superior to a distributional general education requirement in a research
university. An increasing number of institutions are reviewing their general
education programs. What is the most effective pattern of coursework for
students of different ability levels? Is a core curriculum or a set of distributional requirements more appropriate? Jones demonstrates how we can use
the CCAM to provide empirical answers to these questions.

Since the beginning of the twentieth century, and certainly over the
past three decades, the twin objectives of access and equity in higher
education were met largely through the creation of state systems of public
regional four-year colleges and two-year community colleges. While it is
generally reputed that certain colleges and universities are better than
others (for example, that Harvard or Berkeley is superior to California State
University at Hayward or the University of Massachusetts at Boston),
systems of credit transfer between institutions are based on the presumed
equivalence of course credits. In Chapter Four, I examine whether the
credits earned by students at a community college are truly equivalent to
those earned in the lower division of a university. Current models for
articulation rely on comparability of coursework rather than capability of
student learning. One application of the CCAM is the development of an
institutional transfer policy based on the assessment of general learning.

Once the CCAM has been used to identify the coursework patterns
associated with gains in student learning, further analysis can reveal the
types of instruction, reading and writing requirements, and forms of
evaluation used by the faculty who teach courses within each coursework
pattern. In Chapter Five, David S. Guthrie describes a protocol developed
for examining course syllabi and final examinations as indicators of faculty
goals and methods of instruction. Faculty at a research university, a
comprehensive institution, and a liberal arts college were interviewed
regarding their courses that were associated with improvement in student
learning. An intriguing incongruence emerged as interviews, course syllabi,

and examinations from faculty who taught courses associated with student improvement in analytical reasoning were analyzed. While the CCAM data clearly indicate that the students enrolled in these courses showed substantial improvement in analytical reasoning ability, and while faculty viewed themselves as evocative teachers of thinking processes, their goals, modes of instruction, and bases for grading student learning were clearly didactic, with an emphasis on basic understanding of concepts and terminology. Students in these classes were taught and judged by lower-level learning criteria, although faculty envisioned and student outcomes assessment results confirmed improvement in higher-order reasoning skills. Guthrie provides a clearer picture of faculty expectations and faculty practices, on the one hand, and how students are evaluated and the desired outcomes of course planning and teaching, on the other.

In Chapter Six, Elizabeth A. Jones continues the examination of faculty interview data. She analyzes the extent to which faculty attempt to develop cognitive abilities such as analytical reasoning and reading comprehension in students. In general, faculty perceive that their courses help students to develop and enhance different general learned abilities. Jones cites examples from course examinations that reveal the general learned abilities assessed by faculty. She also shows how the use of CCAM to identify which courses consistently produce gains in learning for specific groups of students can effectively serve the goals of curriculum review.

The variation in student backgrounds, preparation, and motivation to attend college suggests that we must give greater attention to students' perceptions of the curriculum in our reform efforts. In the concluding chapter, Susan B. Twombly reports on her interviews with students, giving their stark representations of the lack of clarity and purpose ascribed to general education. She argues that faculty who teach general education courses must understand and enact general education goals in their courses if curriculum reform is to have its intended effects. Recent research on students' and faculty members' perspectives on general education is used as a basis for making recommendations about the objectives of curriculum change.

The research reported in this volume has been generously supported, first, by a grant from the Office of Educational Research and Improvement (OERI), U.S. Department of Education; second, by the Exxon Education Foundation; and, currently, through the National Center on Postsecondary Teaching, Learning, and Assessment, a five-university research consortium housed at Pennsylvania State University and supported by a grant from the Office of Research, OERI.[1] The research would not have been possible without the cooperation of several individuals, including Clifford Adelman at OERI, Ric Garcia and Harry Downs at Clayton State College; Jim Prather at Georgia State University; Stan Ahmann, Camila Benbow, Larry Ebbers, Nak Hon Lee, Stan Johnson, Bob Strahan, and Daphanne

Thomas at Iowa State University; Elizabeth van Patten at Mills College; Larry Metzger and Amy Rubenstein at Ithaca College; David Oehler at Northwest Missouri State University; and Sally Mahoney, Michele Marincovich, and Dean Namboothri at Stanford University. While the authors are indebted to these sponsors and individuals, the analyses and interpretations presented here remain solely those of the authors.

James L. Ratcliff
Editor

Note

1. The National Center on Postsecondary Teaching, Learning, and Assessment (NCTLA) is funded by the U. S. Department of Educational Research and Improvement (OERI), Grant R117G10037. The opinions in this volume do not necessarily reflect the position or policy of OERI, and no official endorsement should be inferred.

JAMES L. RATCLIFF is professor of higher education and director of the Center for the Study of Higher Education at Pennsylvania State University, University Park. He also is executive director of the National Center on Postsecondary Teaching, Learning, and Assessment, and editor of the Journal of General Education.

A new analytical model links student assessment with curriculum reform.

What We Can Learn from Coursework Patterns About Improving the Undergraduate Curriculum

James L. Ratcliff

Most faculty and administrators are committed to improving the quality of undergraduate education. To make improvements, it is necessary to know what students learn in order to decide what ideally they should learn. Assessment plans and programs can monitor institutional performance relative to student learning. Over the past decade, colleges and universities have made substantial efforts to establish student outcomes assessment programs and to revise and reform the undergraduate curriculum. Unfortunately, these two endeavors have not concretely and substantively informed one another.

The 1980s were a decade of examination of the state and quality of education programs. National reports urged faculty and academic leaders to improve baccalaureate programs. The Study Group on the Conditions of Excellence in American Higher Education (1984), formed under the U.S. Department of Education, urged colleges to provide students clear academic direction, standards, and values. It urged researchers to use college student assessment information and to explore the use of student transcripts as resources in understanding more about which subjects students study in college and what they learn. The practical applications, procedures, and techniques of student and curriculum assessment described in the present volume are a direct outcome of those recommendations. Beginning in 1985, we developed specific procedures to determine the

NEW DIRECTIONS FOR HIGHER EDUCATION, no. 80, Winter 1992   © Jossey-Bass Publishers

gains in student learning that were directly associated with enrollment in different patterns of undergraduate coursework.

In February 1985, the Association of American Colleges (AAC) issued the report *Integrity in the College Curriculum: A Report to the Academic Community* (Committee on Redefining the Meaning and Purpose of Baccalaureate Degrees, 1985), which concluded that undergraduate education was in a state of crisis and disarray. The report attacked the "marketplace"-oriented curriculum based solely on student choice, asking "Is the curriculum an invitation to philosophic and intellectual growth or a quick exposure to the skills of a particular vocation?" (p. 2). The report called on colleges and universities to live up to their stated goals for general education and liberal learning by providing a coherent curriculum. For AAC, a coherent curriculum at least entails inquiry, literacy, understanding of numerical data, historical consciousness, science, values, art, international and multicultural experiences, and study of some discipline in depth (Eaton, 1991). AAC reasserted the belief that an undergraduate education should produce learning outcomes common to all students irrespective of their major or minor fields of specialization.

At least three studies have tried to determine what improvements in the college curriculum have been accomplished since 1985. Zemsky (1989) examined thirty-five thousand student transcripts from thirty colleges and universities to determine the shape and substance of the undergraduate curriculum that the students had encountered. Zemsky found that the curriculum continued to lack structure and coherence, that students' enrollment in science and mathematics was quite limited, and that the humanities lacked sequential, developmental patterns of learning. Lynne V. Cheney (1989) analyzed humanities enrollments in colleges and universities to determine if there had been a fundamental change in baccalaureate programs between 1983 and 1989. She found little, if any, change in undergraduate degree requirements. She lamented,

> It is possible to graduate now, as it was five years ago, from *more* than 80 percent of our institutions of higher education without taking a course in American history. In 1988–89, it is possible to earn a bachelor's degree from:
>
> • 37 percent of the nation's colleges and universities without taking any course in history;
> • 45 percent without taking a course in American or English literature;
> • 62 percent without taking a course in philosophy;
> • 77 percent without studying a foreign language [Cheney, 1989, p. 5].

Not only was their little evidence of increased structure and rigor to the curriculum during this time period, there was also evidence that the curriculum was not having much impact on student learning. Astin (1991), in a national study of student transcripts, general education requirements, and student test scores and self-reports found no relationship between any general education curriculum structure and improvement in student learning.

There were strident calls in these national reports and studies to improve undergraduate education, and colleges and universities did not remain idle. During the past decade, more than 90 percent of colleges and universities have engaged in some kind of revision or reform of their undergraduate curriculum (Gaff, 1989). The American Council on Education repeatedly reported in *Campus Trends* (El-Khawas, 1988, 1990) that most colleges and universities were engaged in curriculum reform. These efforts led Eaton (1991, pp. 61, 63) to raise some rather uncomfortable questions about this flurry of activity:

> From a negative point of view, one can point to little in the way of completed curricular modifications or, more important, changes in student performance that . . . emerged . . . as the 1980's ended. Worse, one might view the decade . . . as an essentially unimportant ten-year saga during which the higher-education community continued an apparently endless and unproductive dialogue with itself on academic issues as opposed to engaging in construction action. . . .
> . . . Did institutional descriptions of academic reform fail to focus on those intended to benefit but, instead, confused expectations of student performance with descriptions of faculty involvement?

There has not been a meaningful and substantive connection between undergraduate curriculum content and improved student learning. The increased national attention given to improved student performance and stronger academic direction, standards, and values demands that we make more substantive links between what students study in college and gains in their learning. This volume offers a model for linking general education curriculum and student outcomes assessment. Before I describe this unique model, and before the contributors to this volume show how it can be used to answer tough questions of academic policy and curriculum reform, we first must examine why faculty and administrators are focusing more attention on the assessment of student outcomes.

Impetus for Assessment

A variety of both external and internal factors are compelling institutions not only to consider assessment but also to formalize plans and take specific actions to measure the educational impact of an institution on its students. One group of external factors involves state initiatives. Dissatisfaction with student learning has led an increasing number of states to expect colleges and universities to implement student assessment programs. Earlier state policies toward assessment took a decentralized approach, allowing institutions to develop their own systems of assessment. However, state policy makers are becoming increasingly dissatisfied with assessment programs that do not improve student learning. The result has been new state proposals for common student outcomes testing (Ewell, 1991). Some states have already adopted formal assessment requirements, and many other states are moving in this direction. Every student in Florida who is preparing to receive an associate's degree from a two-year institution or who plans to become a junior in a four-year institution is required by the state to take the College Level Academic Skills Test. Since 1979, Tennessee has based part of its public college and university funding on student assessment results. Colleges and universities in Tennessee test seniors in general education and in their chosen majors, survey alumni, and use the results of assessment activities to guide improvements at the institutions (Banta and others, 1990).

Another set of external factors is composed of accreditation organizations. Most of the six regional accreditation associations have begun to incorporate outcomes assessment as a criterion for institutional approval. The North Central Association of Colleges and Universities has conducted regional seminars on assessment and prepared a workbook to aid in the evaluation of institutional effectiveness and student achievement. In addition, accreditation bodies that approve programs in the disciplines are beginning to include outcomes assessment in their criteria for approval.

Due to these external factors, institutions often have developed and implemented assessment programs to provide accountability. However, there are also internal factors that have encouraged institutions to undertake assessment activities for the sake of academic improvement. The information gathered from assessments can help reform the curriculum, strengthen academic programs and student services, and, consequently, increase student satisfaction and enhance student recruitment and long-term retention. Using the information from assessment activities, faculty can give specific attention to the need for self-improvement in teaching and evaluating students in their own individual courses. The model described in this volume is focused on assessment for the purpose of academic improvement.

Development of the Coursework Cluster Analysis Model

Assessments describe and document the nature and extent of learning that has occurred. They cannot tell us, however, which courses most consistently produce gains in learning for specific groups of students over time at particular institutions. Such information would be extremely useful.

Knowledge about the degree to which different courses contribute to different learning outcomes would provide a college or university with an empirical basis for curriculum review. Knowledge of such links between coursework and learning would complement faculty wisdom, student evaluation, and other means of appraising the extent to which particular sets and sequences of courses have their intended effects. Such information could also be used to improve the academic advising and guidance that students receive in making course selections (Ratcliff and others, 1990a, 1990b, 1990c, 1990d).

Over the past four years, my colleagues and I have developed a model for linking assessments of the general learning of undergraduates with their coursework (Ratcliff, 1987, 1988, 1989; Ratcliff and others, 1990a, 1990b, 1990c, 1990d; Ratcliff and Jones, 1990, 1991; Jones and Ratcliff, 1990a, 1990b, 1991). This research has proceeded under the rubric of the Differential Coursework Patterns Project, and the model for linking coursework to student assessment has been referred to as the Coursework Cluster Analysis Model (CCAM). Its development and testing was supported, first, by the Office of Educational Research and Improvement of the U.S. Department of Education. Subsequent qualitative validity studies of the Graduate Record Examination (GRE) item types, trend analyses of coursework patterns, and studies of the applicability of the model to curriculum reform, assessment program development, and academic advising have been supported by the Exxon Education Foundation. The CCAM has been tested at six institutions: Stanford and Georgia State universities, and Clayton State, Evergreen State, Mills, and Ithaca colleges. In addition, the CCAM has been applied to student reports of enrollment patterns and American College Test-Comprehensive (ACT-COMP) scores at the University of Tennessee, Knoxville (Pike and Phillippi, 1989). Research on the uses and limitations of the CCAM is continuing as part of the National Longitudinal Study of Student Learning at the National Center on Postsecondary Teaching, Learning, and Assessment.

In the most typical applications, assessment instruments are administered to graduating seniors. Since 1986, we have examined over seventy-two thousand courses appearing on the transcripts of approximately sixteen hundred graduating seniors. Each group of seniors came from a cross section of majors. They also reflected the full range of academic ability, as indicated by their Scholastic Aptitude Test (SAT) scores, for the general population of students at each institution. The results of posttests were compared with the results of corresponding pretests of the same students. Well-known standardized instruments were used: the SAT, GRE, ACT, and ACT-COMP, as well as the Kolb Learning Styles Inventory. Locally constructed measures of student-perceived course difficulty also were used. A great strength of the CCAM and an asset that seems to enhance its acceptability to faculty are that the model is not dependent on instruments supplied by external vendors. It can use a variety of locally developed instruments, tailored to particular needs and extensively employing local judgment. A college, for instance, might administer its own essay examinations to freshmen and seniors, and its own faculty might grade them holistically; so long as the final evaluation, or its subparts, can be translated into a numerical scale, this instrument would be entirely adequate for the purpose of the CCAM.

A common stumbling block in the development of an assessment program is that of determining what form of test or assessment information to use. Curriculum reviewers, reformers, and researchers quickly acknowledge that there is no clear conception of what constitutes general learning. Such recognition emerges regardless of whether it is the college curriculum or the various tests and assessment devices that are being examined. A college that attempts to reach consensus among its constituents either on general education goals or on the "best" measure of general learned abilities will foster heated discussion. The quest for consensus on what should be the common intellectual experience of undergraduates may end in irresolution or, worse, abandonment of the assessment initiative. Instead of searching for the ideal measure of general learning in a college, those charged with assessment can better direct their energies toward the selection of a constellation of assessment means and measures that appear to be appropriate criteria for describing one or more dimensions of the general learning goals of the college.

The CCAM provides a basis for determining the relative extent to which each measure explains general student learning within a given college environment. If we have nine different assessment measures, for example, we can determine what proportion of the variation in student scores is explained by each measure. This information leads to a decision point for the academic leader or faculty committee charged with the development and oversight of the assessment program. If a measure of general learning does not explain much of the variation in student scores, one option is to conclude that the measure is inappropriate to the students and the education program of that particular college or university. In short, the CCAM can assist in the discard of that particular form of evaluation as superfluous and unnecessary. An alternative conclusion is that the institution is not devoting sufficient attention to the type of learning measured. Here, an examination of the assessment instrument relative to the curriculum is called for. Again, the CCAM can point to those courses and classes that were associated with gains in student learning on the measure in question.

Steps in the Coursework Cluster Analysis Model

The CCAM is grounded conceptually to the finding that student learning varies more greatly within institutions than between them. The selection, testing, and adoption of a specific methodology for the analysis of course-work patterns were based also on repeated empirical investigation of the relationship between different patterns of coursework and variation in student learning. In this chapter, I describe the general methodology of the CCAM. The rationale and procedures of cluster analysis are described with reference to its application to the investigation of coursework patterns. Since cluster analysis currently is not widely employed in educational research, I begin this section by contrasting cluster analysis with other statistical methods of potential value in the assessment of student learning.

Previous assessment and transcript analysis studies have used the general linear model and regression analysis (Astin, 1970a, 1970b; Benbow and Stanley, 1983; Pallas and Alexander, 1983; Prather and Smith, 1976a, 1976b). The rationale for the use of regression is based on practical and theoretical justifications. Regression analysis allows maximum design flexibility and is statistically robust. Transcript analyses involve large amounts of data. For example, Prather and Smith (1976b) examined 8,735 student transcripts that collectively contained 189,013 individual course grades. Regression analysis provides an effective technique for presenting the diverse nature of the data while maintaining a consistent analysis rationale. However, the general linear model does not provide a direct means of assessing the additive and temporary aspects of course patterns, that is, course combinations and sequences. Moreover, use of linear regression alone would conceptualize the problem as that of finding the one best fit between students and learning experiences. It would not account for the appropriateness and benefits of different learning experiences for different groups of students.

The term *coursework* is used here to refer to the categorization of the courses in which students enrolled according to the multiple assessment criteria of their general education and liberal learning. It is the systematic and unique way in which a college or university labels and arranges its courses (for example, Honors 101, French 340); that scheme or arrange-ment of classes is already known in a disaggregate form on student transcripts. Identification is the allocation of individual courses to be established in categories on the basis of specific criteria (for example, Biology 205 is classified by many universities as a sophomore-level class in the Department of Biology).

Discriminant analysis is used in the CCAM to test the validity of the groupings and to identify those assessment criteria that tell us most about collegiate learning experiences. Discriminant analysis is a process used to differentiate between groups formed on an a priori basis (see Biglan, 1973, for an example). Discriminant analysis does not discover groups; rather, it identifies a set of characteristics that can significantly differentiate between the groups. The process allows the analyst to allocate new cases to one of the a priori groups with the least amount of error. In contrast, *cluster analysis* recovers groups representing particular patterns from diverse populations (Lorr, 1983; Romesburg, 1984). In the CCAM, cluster analysis is used to classify courses according to student achievement criteria, while discriminant analysis is used to test and provide secondary validation of the cluster groupings and to identify those criteria that significantly differentiate one cluster of coursework from another.

Cluster analysis is sometimes confused with factor analysis. Factor analysis is different from cluster analysis in that the analyst's attention is on the similarity of the variables (attributes). The aim is to identify a small number of dimensions (factors) that can account for individual differences on the various measures or attributes. Thus, the aim of factor analysis is to reduce or consolidate the number of attributes of a variable set, whereas the purpose of a cluster analysis is simply to classify or taxonomize data into groups on the basis of a set of attributes. Cluster analysis refers to a wide variety of techniques used to classify entities into homogeneous subgroups on the basis of their similarities.

The end products of cluster analysis are clusters or pattern sets. Since the exact number and nature of the course patterns is not known in advance, the clustering process is actually technically preclassificatory. In other words, cluster analysis techniques are used to construct a classification scheme for unclassified data sets. In this way, cluster analysis empirically arranges the courses of a college curriculum using student decision-making behavior (as represented on transcripts) as the primary source of information. The courses are classified in a hierarchical dendrogram or tree. The relationship between courses is determined by their similarity on the criteria used in the classification. In this way, the similarity between courses is determined empirically, rather than by arbitrary concepts (for example, life sciences) or levels (for example, freshmen-level survey). This conceptual-empirical approach was selected due to the lack of agreement in the higher education literature on a common research paradigm, model, or philosophy for the organization of coursework (Bergquist, Gould, and Greenberg, 1981; Biglan, 1973; Fuhrman and Grasha, 1983; Gaff, 1983; Rudolph, 1977; Sloan, 1971; Veysey, 1973).

Cluster analysis conforms to the conceptual restrictions placed on the CCAM to assess the effect of coursework patterns on student learning. Cluster analysis provides a statistical procedure for examining coursework using multiple criteria. It can classify different sets of coursework according to different net effects of learning associated with them. It can accommodate both quantitative and qualitative attributes of varying dimensions. Thus, the criterion selected need not be test scores; nominal, ordinal, interval, and ratio data have been successfully used as attributes in cluster analysis (Romesburg, 1984). Cluster analysis uses these attributes to arrive at patterns of coursework independently of any institutionally prescribed a priori distinctions. Therefore, it can test the combinations, sequences, and progressions of courses within the undergraduate curriculum. It leads to the discovery of clusters (or patterns) of coursework in student transcripts, based on the multiple measures of student assessment employed. Since the purpose of the CCAM is to group coursework homogeneously relative to student learning criteria (Lorr, 1983; Romesburg, 1984), cluster analysis serves as the primary methodology for the analytical model.

Overview of the CCAM Steps. There are several steps to using the CCAM. First, student residual scores are derived. A residual score is the difference between the student's actual score on the outcomes assessment measure and the score predicted by the entrance measure used. Next, student transcripts are examined. Courses reported on them are clustered into patterns based on the residual scores of the students who enrolled in them. The resulting coursework patterns are then grouped or classified according to any of a wide variety of student or institutional factors. Patterns can be classified according to factors such as the entering ability level of the student, the type of coursework selected (general education, prerequisites), the campus at which the student enrolled, or the residence facilities housing the students. Adult versus traditional college-age students, commuter versus residential students, and part-time versus full-time students' coursework can be compared. Within systems of higher education with course comparability, transfer schemes, and articulation agreements, the model can be used to determine if coursework associated with students from branch campuses or with transfer students is associated with the same types of improvement in learning as found for students native to the campus.

A Closer Look at the CCAM Steps. The CCAM research design uses official student transcripts and assessment instrument scores as data sources for a sample of graduating senior students. To describe the model and to illustrate how CCAM is executed, I here use the nine item-type categories of the General Test of the GRE as examples of multiple measures of general learned abilities of college seniors. Standardized and non-standardized, locally developed and commercially available assessment instruments and measures can be used with CCAM. In the following example, SAT scores are used as controls for the academic abilities of these students when they first entered college. The student transcripts are used as the unobtrusive record of the sequence of courses in which these seniors enrolled.

The first objective of the CCAM is to determine the extent of student improvement in general learned abilities over the time of their baccalaureate program. To achieve this objective, the residual score of each GRE item type for each student is calculated first; the residual score is the difference between the student's actual score and the score predicted by the student's corresponding SAT score. It is derived by regressing the outcomes measure (in this case, GRE item types) on the entrance measures (in this case, SAT scores). Thus, for each student outcomes measure there is a student residual score for each person in the sample group.

The second objective is to determine patterns of coursework on the student transcripts that are associated with the student score residuals. Cluster analysis gives us these patterns, using student residual scores (GRE item-type residuals) as attributes of the courses in which students enrolled. To achieve this second objective, we create a data matrix where all of the courses to be analyzed are in the columns and all of the assessment measures or criteria are in the rows. Each cell in this matrix is then filled with the appropriate mean course residual score. For example, let us assume that we have student assessment data on writing ability and understanding of scientific knowledge, and a writing sample that has been holistically scored. For the course Introduction to Political Systems, we calculate the mean of residual scores for all students enrolling in it for each of these measures. We do this for Introduction to Political Science and every other course on the students' transcripts that we select to analyze.

Now, with several rows of assessment data, a column for each course analyzed, and a course mean residual score in every cell of the data matrix, we are ready to determine how similarly students who enrolled in different courses performed. The course mean residual score is the metric value that we are going to use to make the comparisons of coursework. To determine how courses are similar to one another in this way, we use the correlation coefficient (Pearson's r) as the indicator of similarity.

Our task is to see how the performance of students in the course Introduction to Political Systems is similar to the performance of students in other courses. However, students take more than one course, so courses taken by a particular group of students will cluster together. That is because the course mean residuals for each assessment measure should look about the same for all of the courses taken by this group of students.

So, if we correlate the writing sample score of Introduction to Political Systems with the sociology course Mass Behavior, then the correlation will be high if students for both courses showed comparable improvement on that measure. What we are doing, then, is creating a second matrix to record our correlation coefficient. In this matrix, all of the rows are the courses analyzed, and all of the columns are a duplicate listing of all of the courses. Each cell contains the coefficient representing the extent to which each course is related to all other courses on all the assessment criteria. Obviously, the greater the assessment criteria, the more precision in establishing the relationship. Construction of these two data matrices, the raw data matrix and the course resemblance matrix, may seem like a lot of work. Fortunately, use of a computer with popular statistical programs, such as SPSS and SAS, makes the task easy. We do not even see these matrices as they are calculated at lightning speed as we move along performing the CCAM cluster analysis.

Once the resemblance matrix indicating the proportional relationship of courses is established, a clustering method is selected and executed to arrange a tree or dendrogram of courses related by the student score gains. Next, we conduct a discriminant analysis on the resulting clusters of coursework. The discriminant analysis tells us the extent to which the courses have been correctly classified according to the assessment criteria, which of the assessment criteria were correlated with particular discriminant functions, and which coursework clusters were associated with the improvement of student learning according to which assessment criteria. From the discriminant analysis, an association can be inferred between coursework patterns (clusters) and the assessment criteria (student score residuals on the multiple measures of learning). The cluster analysis procedure groups courses frequently chosen by students according to the strength of their associated effect on the student score gains.

The CCAM classifies the most frequently enrolled courses according to their associated effect on student improvement in learning. The procedure classifies courses according to a ratio index of similarity to other courses. This procedure is designed to examine those courses in which most students enroll. Thus, the analysis is limited to only a fraction of all of the courses in a college curriculum. For example, in the historical data base used in model building and testing, a 5 percent sample of student transcripts enabled an examination of only 5 percent of the courses appearing on those transcripts (the percentage of courses enrolling five or more students from the sample group). However, the courses examined in that 5 percent corresponded closely to those courses identified as meeting the college's distributional degree requirements in general education. The quantitative procedures and techniques are described in greater detail in Ratcliff, Jones, and Hoffman (1992).

The linking of coursework to assessment results is critical given the diversity of the undergraduate curriculum today. Most colleges and universities have an expansive curriculum representing the explosion of knowledge, diversity of students, and modes of inquiry that characterize higher education in the twentieth century. Given this observation about the undergraduate curriculum, we find that up to 20 percent of the courses are not to be found on the transcripts of the preceding or following year's graduating seniors. The reason for this is that annual course schedules do not represent all of the courses found in the college catalogue. Certain courses are given on a one-time experimental basis, and some are cancelled due to lack of enrollment. Typically, the undergraduate student chooses thirty-five to forty-five courses to fulfill the baccalaureate degree requirements from a list of twenty-five hundred to five thousand courses at a large research university or from eight hundred to fifteen hundred courses at a liberal arts college. Therefore, what students learn and how much they learn at a given institution varies from year to year based on variations in course offerings and student course selections. This variation in student learning within a single institution often is greater than the variation in student learning across institutions.

Findings from Research Based on the Coursework Cluster Analysis Model

Students who take different coursework learn different content, cognitive skills, values, and attitudes. Student learning varies greatly in complex institutions of higher education because of their broad arrays of curriculum offerings. Critical to the success of general and liberal education for students in these institutions is some means for recognizing curriculum diversity and its effects. Thus, the more complex the curriculum offerings, the greater is the challenge to determine the relationship between coursework taken and learning achieved.

Based on measures of general learning and the transcripts of graduating seniors, the coursework taken by students who showed large gains in these measures can be identified. In our research, we found that different patterns and sequences of coursework produced different types of gains in learning. For example, course sequences in a wide range of disciplines such as business, biology, and philosophy were associated with gains in student learning in analytical reasoning. Student improvement in mathematics was associated with coursework in economics, business, music, physical therapy, mathematics, and quantitative methods in management. Student gains in reading comprehension were associated with coursework in marketing, accounting, management, music, and history. These findings and relationships are described and illustrated more fully in Jones (this volume, Chapter Three), where the CCAM is used to test the viability of a core curriculum to engender improvement in students' learned abilities.

Consistently, we have found that students who take different coursework learn different things and develop different abilities. There are two lessons form this research. First, the courses that students take in college have a bearing on what they learn. Second, the structure of general education in the institutions that we examined did not produce a profound effect on the types of learning that we examined. While the current general requirements of American colleges and universities may show little effect on the development of general learned abilities of students (Astin, 1991), the specific coursework taken by those students does have an effect (Ratcliff and Jones, 1990, 1991). We believe that improvements in student learned abilities can be achieved by revising undergraduate curriculum experiences to emulate the coursework clusters, patterns, and sequences taken by those students who show large gains in student learning. Here lies the potential power of assessment to guide and monitor the reform of undergraduate education.

What the Coursework Cluster Analysis Model Can Do

The CCAM provides a way for faculty and administrators to make more substantive links between what students study in college and what they learn. It suggests that an ideal coursework pattern is one in which what is to be learned is well matched to the background, preparation, and interests of the learners. The more diverse the student population, the greater is the need for alternative coursework patterns to fulfill the general education requirements.

The model and method of analysis defined in this volume permit a college or university to achieve several tasks of curriculum reform: determine which assessment measures best describe the kinds of learning that take place among students at the institution, determine which parts of the curriculum are currently not monitored or described by the present assessment methods and measures, determine which patterns of coursework are associated with which kinds of learning and with which groups of students, determine the extent to which transfer students benefit from the same or different general education coursework as that taken by students who began their baccalaureate program at the same institution, determine the extent to which a core curriculum or a distributional requirement produces the greatest gains in learning among different groups of undergraduates at the same institution, and determine which course sequences contribute to general education and liberal learning and which do not. The CCAM has limitations as well. It is designed for assessment of general education and liberal learning, not learning within the major; those institutions that have a distribution plan of general education in which students have a fairly wide range of curriculum choices to fulfill the requirements for their baccalaureate; the identification of coursework *associated* with improvement in student learning in general education and liberal learning. It does not tell us that coursework *caused* the learning. Subsequent research and analysis are required to determine which factors contributed to that learning.

Advantages to Assessing Coursework Pattern

The CCAM provides a number of advantages and benefits in the assessment of general education. First, the model can use multiple measures of assessment, thereby allowing for a broader picture of student learning than any one measure can paint. It provides institutions with information regarding the extent of variation in student assessment results that is explained by any one of the measures used. This information can be helpful in a number of ways. Faculty and administrators need not decide on an ideal set of assessment measures. The extent to which such measures may overlap in describing student learning can be identified. The mix of assessment measures appropriate to the goals of the institution and the characteristics of the student population can be continuously monitored. When students show small amounts of growth on an indicator of student learning, the college or university can either develop strategies for improving student learning in the area identified or else discard the measure as inappropriate to the institution and its students.

Efforts to assess general education and liberal learning can become quickly bogged down in discussions over which measures, indicators, or examinations to use. Faculty feel pressured to commit to a set of measures that may not accurately reflect their visions of the goals of general education. By using multiple measures and by leaving the process of choosing measures open to continuous revision and updating, the college or university can proceed to develop a rational, cogent, and informative assessment plan. Eaton (1991, p. 66) has written about tensions that emerge over the discussion of the desired outcomes of general education and the desirability of such a contingency approach: "These tensions emerge when we are either unwilling or unable to commit some defensible approach to general education for fear that our commitment will be found lacking in some way. Waiting around for the ideal general education scenario, however, serves little purpose and harms students even more than a general education effort that possesses some flaws."

If a general education innovation holds promise to enhance student learning in some way, then there should be a means to ascertain whether or not that improvement has occurred. Linked analysis of assessment and enrollment data holds the promise of identifying when and, more important, under what circumstances the general education curriculum has been improved. The CCAM provides useful information to the college or university about the mix of assessment measures that reflects what the students learn and what the institution intends to teach them.

The model can provide concrete useful information about the curriculum to guide reform efforts. It is a tool ideally suited to institutions of higher education with a distributional general education requirements and a wide array of programs, electives, and majors. From a catalogue of hundreds or thousands of courses, the CCAM can identify the courses taken by students who showed the greatest improvement in learning. For example, if one of the assessment measures that a college selects is a test of analytical reasoning, then the CCAM can identify those groups of courses taken by students who showed significant improvement in that area of general learning.

The finding that different courses engender different types of learning is actually a corollary to a larger, more important research finding affirmed in our research but best described by Pascarella and Terenzini (1991). They describe and analyze twenty years of research indicating that *differences in student learning are far greater within institutions than between them.* Given this finding, it stands to reason that students taking different coursework and having different extracurricular experiences should show differences in subject matter learned, in the type and extent of their general cognitive development, and in their values and attitudes toward learning.

This finding that variation in student learning is greater within institutions than between them also means that one intellectual shoe does not fit all freshmen feet. The efficacy of a single set of courses, a core, in fostering the intellectual development of college students can be easily examined using assessment results. Likewise, the efficacy of specific combinations and sequences of coursework can be scrutinized relative to the long-term learning gains of students. The specific learning preparation, interests, and outcomes of different groups of students can be examined, whether they are low ability, high ability, transfer students, or students from specific curricula or majors.

The student population can be subdivided by ability, by gender, race, or ethnicity, or by major. Then the CCAM can identify if the coursework associated with gains in learning among the total group is the same as that for the subgroups. Curriculum planners and curriculum committees can readily use this information. Courses in the general education sequence that are not associated with gains in student learning can be revised, enhanced, or dropped. Courses outside the general education requirements that contribute to gains in student learning can be included in the general education curriculum.

The model can also produce information that leads to better academic advising, since it links the coursework that students take with their improvement in learning. Students can choose from lists of courses taken by others with similar backgrounds and abilities —others who showed gains in performance and learning. This procedure takes advising beyond the mere listing of formal degree requirements. As more data are amassed, increasingly greater precision is generated in the linking of coursework and student learning. The CCAM may even be amenable to the development of a microcomputer-based advising system utilizing a relational data base of prior students' course-taking patterns and assessment results. Such a computer-based advising system would yield an array of effective coursework tailored to the abilities and interests of individual students and within the parameters of institutional degree requirements. In subsequent chapters, we explore and exemplify how the linking of curriculum information (transcripts, catalogue studies, course syllabi, and examinations) with student outcomes assessment data can guide undergraduate curriculum reform.

References

Astin, A. W. "The Methodology of Research on College Impact, Part 1." *Sociology of Education*, 1970a, 43, 223–254.

Astin, A. W. "The Methodology of Research on College Impact, Part 2." *Sociology of Education*, 1970b, 43, 437–450.

Astin, A. W. *Assessment for Excellence: The Philosophy and Practice of Assessment and Evaluation in Higher Education.* New York: Macmillan, 1991.

Banta, T., and others. *Bibliography of Assessment Instruments.* Knoxville, Tenn.: Center for Assessment Research and Development, University of Tennessee, 1990.

Benbow, C. P., and Stanley, J. C. "Differential Course-Taking Hypothesis Revisited." *American Educational Research Journal,* 1983, *20* (4), 469–573.

Bergquist, W. H., Gould, R. A., and Greenberg, E. M. *Designing Undergraduate Education: A Systematic Guide.* San Francisco: Jossey-Bass, 1981.

Biglan, A. "The Characteristics of Subject Matter in Different Academic Areas." *Journal of Applied Psychology,* 1973, *57* (3), 195–203.

Cheney, L. V. *50 Hours: A Core Curriculum for College Students.* Washington, D.C.: National Endowment for the Humanities, 1989.

Committee on Redefining the Meaning and Purpose of Baccalaureate Degrees. Association of American Colleges. *Integrity in the College Curriculum: A Report to the Academic Community.* Washington, D.C.: Association of American Colleges, 1985.

Eaton, J. S. *The Unfinished Agenda: Higher Education and the 1980s.* New York: Macmillan, 1991.

El-Khawas, E. *Campus Trends, 1988.* Higher Education Panel Reports, No. 77. Washington, D.C.: American Council on Education, 1988.

El-Khawas, E. *Campus Trends, 1990.* Higher Education Panel Reports, No. 80. Washington, D.C.: American Council on Education, 1990.

Ewell, P. "Assessment and Public Accountability: Back to the Future." *Change,* 1991, *23,* 12–17.

Fuhrman, B., and Grasha, A. *A Practical Handbook for College Teachers.* Boston: Little, Brown, 1983.

Gaff, J. G. *General Education Today: A Critical Analysis of Controversies, Practices, and Reforms.* San Francisco: Jossey-Bass, 1983.

Gaff, J. G. "General Education at the Decade's End: The Need for a Second Wave of Reform." *Change,* 1989, *21,* 11–19.

Jones, E. A., and Ratcliff, J. L. "Effective Coursework Patterns and Faculty Perceptions of the Development of General Learned Abilities." Paper presented at the annual meeting of the Association for the Study of Higher Education, Portland, Oregon, November 1990a.

Jones, E. A., and Ratcliff, J. L. "Is a Core Curriculum Best for Everybody? The Effect of Different Patterns of Coursework on the General Education of High and Low Ability Students." Paper presented at the annual meeting of the American Educational Research Association, Boston, April 1990b.

Jones, E. A., and Ratcliff, J. L. "Which General Education Curriculum Is Better: Core Curriculum or the Distributional Requirement?" *Journal of General Education,* 1991, *40,* 69–101.

Lorr, M. *Cluster Analysis for Social Scientists: Techniques for Analyzing and Simplifying Complex Blocks of Data.* San Francisco: Jossey-Bass, 1983.

Pallas, A. M., and Alexander, K. L. "Sex Differences in Quantitative SAT Performance: New Evidence on the Differential Coursework Hypothesis." *American Educational Research Journal,* 1983, *20* (2), 165–182.

Pascarella, E. T., and Terenzini, P. T. *How College Affects Students: Findings and Insights from Twenty Years of Research.* San Francisco: Jossey-Bass, 1991.

Pike, G. R., and Phillippi, R. H. "Generalizability of the Differential Coursework Methodology: Relationships Between Self-Reported Coursework and Performance on the ACT-COMP Exam." *Research in Higher Education,* 1989, *30* (3), 245–260.

Prather, J. E., and Smith, G. *Faculty Grading Patterns.* Atlanta: Office of Institutional Planning, Georgia State University, 1976a.

Prather, J. E., and Smith, G. *Undergraduate Grades by Course in Relation to Student Ability Levels, Programs of Study, and Longitudinal Trends.* Atlanta: Office of Institutional Planning, Georgia State University, 1976b.

Ratcliff, J. L. *The Effect of Differential Coursework Patterns on General Learned Abilities of College Students: Application of the Model to a Historical Database of Student Transcripts.* Report on Task No. 3 for the U.S. Department of Education, Office of Educational Research and Improvement, Contract No. OERI-R-86-0016. Ames: Iowa State University, 1987.

Ratcliff, J. L. "The Development of a Cluster Analytic Model for Determining the Associated Effects of Coursework Patterns on Student Learning." Paper presented at the annual meeting of the American Educational Research Association, New Orleans, April 1988.

Ratcliff, J. L. "Determining the Effects of Different Coursework Patterns on the General Student Learning at Four Colleges and Universities." Paper presented at the annual meeting of the American Educational Research Association, San Francisco, March 1989.

Ratcliff, J. L., and Jones, E. A. "General Learning at a Women's College." Paper presented at the annual meeting of the Association for the Study of Higher Education, Portland, Oregon, November 1990.

Ratcliff, J. L., and Jones, E. A. "Are Common Course Numbering and a Core Curriculum Valid Indicators in the Articulation of General Education Credits Among Transfer Students?" Paper presented at the annual meeting of the American Educational Research Association, Chicago, April 1991.

Ratcliff, J. L., Jones, E. A., and Hoffman, S. *Handbook on Linking Assessment and General Education.* University Park: National Center for Postsecondary Teaching, Learning, and Assessment, Pennsylvania State University, 1992.

Ratcliff, J. L., and others. *Development and Testing of a Cluster-Analytic Model for Identifying Coursework Patterns Associated with General Learned Abilities of College Students: Final Report on Stanford University Samples Nos. 1–2.* Prepared for the U.S. Department of Education, Office of Educational Research and Improvement, Contract No. OERI-R-86-0016. Ames: Iowa State University, 1990a.

Ratcliff, J. L., and others. *Development and Testing of a Cluster-Analytic Model for Identifying Coursework Patterns Associated with General Learned Abilities of College Students: Final Report on Ithaca College Samples Nos. 1–2.* Prepared for the U.S. Department of Education, Office of Educational Research and Improvement, Contract No. OERI-R-86-0016. Ames: Iowa State University, 1990b.

Ratcliff, J. L., and others. *Development and Testing of a Cluster-Analytic Model for Identifying Coursework Patterns Associated with General Learned Abilities of College Students: Final Report on Ithaca College Sample No. 3.* Prepared for the Exxon Education Foundation. University Park: Center for the Study of Higher Education, Pennsylvania State University, 1990c.

Ratcliff, J. L., and others. *Development and Testing of a Cluster-Analytic Model for Identifying Coursework Patterns Associated with General Learned Abilities of College Students: Final Report on Mills College Samples Nos. 1–2.* Prepared for the U.S. Department of Education, Office of Educational Research and Improvement, Contract No. OERI-R-86-0016. University Park: Center for the Study of Higher Education, Pennsylvania State University, 1990d.

Romesburg, H. C. *Cluster Analysis for Researchers.* Belmont, Calif.: Lifelong Learning, 1984.

Rudolph, F. *Curriculum: A History of the American Undergraduate Course of Study Since 1636.* San Francisco: Jossey-Bass, 1977.

Sloan, D. "Harmony, Chaos, and Consensus: The American College Curriculum." *Teachers College Record,* 1971, 73, 221–251.

Study Group on the Conditions of Excellence in American Higher Education. National Institute of Education. *Involvement in Learning: Realizing the Potential of American Higher Education.* Washington, D.C.: Government Printing Office, 1984.

Veysey, L. "Stability and Experiment in the American Undergraduate Curriculum." In C. Kaysen (ed.), *Content and Context: Essays on College Education.* New York: McGraw-Hill, 1973.

Zemsky, R. *Structure and Coherence: Measuring the Undergraduate Curriculum.* Washington, D.C.: Association of American Colleges, 1989.

JAMES L. RATCLIFF is professor of higher education and director of the Center for the Study of Higher Education at Pennsylvania State University, University Park. He also is executive director of the National Center on Postsecondary Teaching, Learning, and Assessment, and editor of the Journal of General Education.

Catalogues can be useful in tracking curriculum scope, content, and change.

Using Catalogues to Track Institutional Viability and Change

Marilyn J. Amey

Academic administrators and faculty are regularly faced with the task of assessing undergraduate curricula for evidence of viability and change. The size, scope, and variation of the curriculum within any given college or university adds to the challenge of finding an assessment model or format that will provide sufficient and appropriate information for answering pertinent curriculum questions. Conceptual models for studying the college curriculum take many forms, based on varying definitions, intended outcomes, and research objectives. In this chapter, I look closely at the institutional-structural approach to curriculum assessment, which focuses on the structure of the formal curriculum. A description of institutional-structural models is provided, with particular attention placed on catalogue studies as one type of application of these models to formal curricula. Several catalogue studies are reviewed for the kind of curriculum information provided and the methodological concerns identified by the researchers. Finally, I discuss the utility of this approach to curriculum study and the implications for administrators and researchers of using catalogue studies for tracking institutional innovation and change.

Institutional-Structural Models of Curriculum Research

There are at least two broad categories of conceptual models for studying the college curriculum: institutional-structural and student development oriented. Institutional-structural models examine the formal and informal organizational structures of institutions and their components as related to curriculum. Dressel and DeLisle (1969), Biglan (1973), Conrad (1978),

New Directions for Higher Education, no. 80, Winter 1992   © Jossey-Bass Publishers

Levine (1978), Bergquist, Gould, and Greenberg (1981), and Toombs, Fairweather, Chen, and Amey (1989) are examples of studies that can be characterized as institution-structural models of the college curriculum. In contrast, student-development-oriented models examine relationships and interactions that impact students' cognitive and general personal development and maturation. Alexander Astin and his colleagues remain at the forefront of this type of investigation (Astin, 1970, 1977; Hurtado, Astin, and Dey, 1991), as well as Pascarella (1985), the National Center for Research to Improve Postsecondary Teaching and Learning (McKeachie, Pintrich, Lin, and Smith, 1986), and the National Center on Postsecondary Teaching, Learning, and Assessment. Both institutional-structural and student-development-oriented curriculum models provide assessment information that can increase our understanding of the college curriculum and inform our practice. Similarly, both types of models are limited in the range of questions that they can answer, in part due to the constraints of their research designs and methodologies. The focus of this chapter is on the institutional-structural curriculum models that primarily address the nature and organization of the specified or formal curriculum at a given institution.

When using institutional-structural curriculum models, we can focus the analysis on the institutional level, or, more narrowly, on specifications designated at the school, departmental, or program level. Institutional-structural curriculum models can be used to examine written goals, objectives, rules, and regulations of the academic unit of analysis as related to curriculum. These models assume that curricula can be described in terms of various combinations of general education requirements, major requirements, and electives. All begin with an examination of how the curriculum is put together and functions, and then they diverge from there.

Curriculum studies falling within the institutional-structural conceptual rubric are useful for the discovery of various aspects of the formal curriculum. They can uncover the structure of innovation and variation in the depth and breadth of curriculum in the major and in general education, elective versus prescription components, and the abundance or scarcity of course offerings. Such studies identify courses that a student "should take" based on institutional philosophy as well as values placed on curriculum components that are reflected in program and degree requirements. Institutional-structural studies can provide a snapshot of the curriculum or they can demonstrate trends over time.

Institutional-structural curriculum studies in general do not provide information about student characteristics or the interactive nature of the learning process. Because they focus on public statements about the structure of the curriculum, institutional-structural studies do not reveal individual faculty or administrative belief systems about education and learning, instructional methodologies, or the substance of what is taught.

This limitation does not suggest that the structure of the formal curriculum is totally separate from belief systems about education and learning. In fact, there are many ways in which institutional and departmental belief systems are conveyed through the documentation of the formal curriculum. For instance, beliefs about subject and sequence in the curriculum are embedded in presumptions about a core curriculum, in four levels of study (freshman through senior), in the practice of assigning course numbers that correspond with those levels of study, and in the designation of course prerequisites. These artifacts of beliefs systems can all be captured through an institutional-structural study. How the artifacts are interpreted by faculty and students and their impact on learning and instruction remain hidden with this approach to curriculum study.

Institutional-structural curriculum studies show course offering trends, but in isolation they do not contribute to our awareness of student course-taking behavior, which is part of the informal curriculum. Institutional-structural studies indicate an abundance or scarcity of coursework and can demonstrate the development or elimination of programs, majors, and so on over time; but the research does not provide an understanding of the intent behind these changes or the meaning that they represent and convey to academic constituents. Finally, course sequencing can be established through formal curriculum data, but most actual course content is not found in sources such as college catalogues, especially if course descriptions are not presented with course titles and numbers.

Curriculum Research Using College Catalogues

Catalogue studies are considered one kind of institutional-structural approach to curriculum analysis because the college or program catalogues present the primary formal statements of an institution's academic program. They are available to the public and are therefore unobtrusive data sources and are intended to represent at least a rudimentary consensus of where the faculty stand in terms of the curriculum. Catalogues do not present the whole story of the curriculum, its influence, or intended outcomes, but the descriptions of academic programs found in college catalogues constitute a fundamental body of information, prepared with care and confirmed by publication. The course titles and numbers presented throughout the college catalogue demonstrate the sheer volume of classes comprising an institution's curriculum. When examined across disciplines, across an institutional setting, or across colleges and universities, catalogues provide indications of the academic climate of postsecondary education (Toombs, Fairweather, Chen, and Amey, 1989). When examined across time, catalogues reveal trends in and rates of curriculum innovation and, to some degree, institutional, departmental, and program priorities.

Most often, catalogue studies involve systematic reviews of college and program catalogues based on a set of hypotheses or research questions related to the curriculum. From a college catalogue, it is possible to collect course titles and numbers, program and course descriptions, combinations of required and elective courses, requirements of majors, and descriptive information about curriculum intent found in mission statements. These components of the formal curriculum can then be used to answer a variety of curriculum questions about topics such as the evolution of a particular academic program or the current composition of a specific major. Catalogue studies are often narrow in scope, such as single-institution studies, single disciplines across institutions, or sample sizes ranging from five to three hundred for institutionwide comparisons. This narrow focus is due in part to the data collection process, which usually involves collecting and carefully reading entire catalogues in order to gather sufficient information for appropriate analysis. The Career Guidance Foundation of San Diego operates a microfiche service on subscription for most libraries that allows for easier access to catalogues (Toombs, Fairweather, Chen, and Amey, 1989). Reading catalogues is a time-intensive activity, especially on microfiche, due to the format, organization, and sheer volume of curriculum information that is not always consistently presented throughout college catalogues.

Over time, many researchers and administrators have come to rely on college catalogues as primary data sources for their studies of curriculum issues. A review of some of these studies reveals that catalogues have often been effectively used to illuminate three aspects of the formal curriculum in particular: the development of specific academic areas, the change in general higher education curriculum offerings over specified periods of time, and the development of course classification systems. The studies rely on course descriptions, course titles, and degree requirements across institutional levels for data.

Specific Academic Areas. One of the most frequent uses of catalogue studies is to examine specific academic disciplines. Becan-McBride (1980), Boysen (1979), Fosdick (1984), LoGuidice (1983), and Tenopir (1985) are among those who have used catalogues to study the status of particular academic areas. Gillespie and Cameron (1986) and Grace (1985) used catalogues to look at change over time in various academic disciplines. In each case, the primary data were derived from analysis of course titles and course descriptions found in college catalogues. Boysen (1979) used common words and phrases, sorted into a priori categories, to indicate the degree to which an international perspective had permeated institutional programs. Fosdick (1984) took a similar approach to study the educational impact of information science on library science curricula. Fosdick's research was based on course titles and descriptions found in catalogues because he believed in their objectivity over verbal or written survey data. Tenopir (1985) followed much the same methodological approach to catalogue research, assigning courses to predetermined categories via catalogue course descriptions and titles. Tenopir used departmental studies in the sorting process as well. Catalogues were again chosen as the source of data because of their unobtrusiveness in charting the development of a specialization in information science.

Instead of focusing only on course titles and descriptions, Becan-McBride (1980) used catalogues of medical technology programs to examine program characteristics such as course requirements, nature of the program, degree earned, and accreditation. Catalogue data were supplemented with information provided through institutionally developed brochures. In a similar vein, Gillespie and Cameron (1986) drew from other institutionally public documents such as textbooks and national convention programs to supplement their catalogue data in a study of the development of the teaching of acting on college campuses. Grace (1985) used catalogues to gather and compare program hours and courses within and outside higher education curricula to determine the extent of professionalization of the field. She then moved beyond a study of the formal curriculum to the informal curriculum through the use of program handbooks and student transcripts.

In addition to what these studies showed about the advent of specific disciplines through catalogue research, they also revealed several weaknesses inherent to the use of catalogues as primary data sources. For example, catalogue studies often rely on course titles for tracking the evolution of programs and curriculum areas. Yet, departments and institutions often use different titles to represent similar courses, and vice versa. The variation in intra- and interinstitutional vernacular make data gathering based on course titles more difficult and more time-consuming and the analysis more subjective than the tasks at first appear. These dilemmas are magnified when research teams are used for data gathering because the opportunity is greater for multiple interpretations and classifications of vague or conflicting course titles. A priori classification designations and decision rules for dealing with ambiguity in catalogue phrasing are common strategies used in this kind of research to assist with data collection. Judgmental categorizations are still often required of individual investigators. When more than one investigator is involved, initial training in the reading of catalogues and, later, spot checking, conferencing on difficult decisions, and so on may be required for maintaining interrater reliability.

Change over Time. Beyond using college catalogues to study specific academic disciplines, researchers can also use catalogue data to examine higher education curriculum issues such as broad curriculum change and the emphasis on general education. Hefferlin (1969), Dressel and DeLisle (1969), Blackburn and others (1976), and Toombs, Fairweather, Chen, and Amey (1989) are four such studies.

Hefferlin's (1969) study produced a model for analyzing curriculum change through an examination of catalogue data in five areas: program majors, areas of concentration, requirements within majors, degree requirements for graduation, and general curriculum regulations. His institutional vitality model was based on the proportion of courses dropped or noticeably altered in departments where the number of courses increased or decreased. By collecting catalogue data over a five-year period, Hefferlin was able to chart the expansion or decline of components of the curriculum.

Studies following the Hefferlin work tended to focus primarily, if not exclusively, on change over time in the general education component of institutional curricula. Change in these studies was basically defined on the basis of breadth and depth of the curriculum over time, as represented by the percentage of course requirements comprising general education (breadth) and the percentage representing the major (depth). For example, Dressel and DeLisle (1969) provided a baseline ten-year curriculum study of 322 colleges and universities that eventually would be replicated, at least in part, two more times in the next twenty years. The original research found a decline in the specificity of general education requirements across institutions, a wide variation in the course and credit requirements of academic majors, and an increase in the proportion of electives permitted in fulfilling degree requirements over the time frame of the study.

Blackburn and others (1976) designed their study, in part, to replicate Dressel and DeLisle's work, examining the status of undergraduate curricula from 1967 to 1974. Blackburn and his colleagues found that the proportion of coursework committed to the academic major changed very little when compared to the data from Dressel and DeLisle's study. During the period studied by Blackburn and his colleagues, there was a decrease in general education course requirements that resulted in an increase in permissible elective credits. In addition, Blackburn and his colleagues included transcript analysis as a measure of student course-taking behavior. In this way, they were able to compare stated degree requirements (the formal curriculum) with actual student course-taking behavior (the informal curriculum). The final replication of Dressel and DeLisle's work was a study of change in general education by Toombs, Fairweather, Chen, and Amey (1989). Using seven hundred 1986–1987 college catalogues, they look specifically at degree, general education, and major requirements. They also included descriptive information from curriculum mission statements found in the catalogues. The research showed an increase in the proportion of the curriculum devoted to general education in the time period following the report of Blackburn and his colleagues, whereas overall degree requirements remained relatively consistent between 1976 and 1987.

Each of the replication studies acknowledged the difficulties in using catalogues as primary data sources described originally by Dressel and

DeLisle (1969). Catalogues are often poorly organized, inaccurate, ambiguously written, and intra- and interinstitutionally inconsistent. For example, different sections of college catalogues sometimes provide contradictory lists of general education requirements. Terms such as *required, core,* and *elective,* while seemingly explicit, often have different meanings within and across institutions. Methodologically, each of the studies followed Dressel and DeLisle took a different strategy to overcome the limitations of catalogues, including the development of an institutional vitality model by Hefferlin (1969), the use of transcript analysis by Blackburn and others (1976), and the large sample size and descriptor analysis used by Toombs, Fairweather, Chen, and Amey (1989). The combination of transcript analysis and catalogue data used by Blackburn and his colleagues made perhaps the most viable connections between the formal and informal curricula, yet the process of transcript analysis also proved to be slow and expensive. The advent of more sophisticated computer programs since 1976, such as the Academic Requirements Tracking System, may alleviate some of the concerns associated with the use of transcript analyses in future institutional-structural curriculum studies.

Course Coding and Classification. A second use of catalogue data has been to develop classification schemes. Catalogue data sometimes have been used to address the structural consistency of curricula across institutions, in addition to informing practitioners about trends in the internal structure of the curriculum. Two studies have used college catalogues in this way to develop course classification systems at the state and national levels. Waggaman (1980) looked at the effect of various forms of credit and non-credit designations that made transfer among Florida institutions particularly problematic. On a national level, the Classification of Secondary School Courses Project of the National Center for Education Statistics (1982) used course descriptions from high school catalogues to develop a nationwide inventory of secondary school courses to assist with the coding of high school transcripts. Both studies used catalogue data to develop classification schemes that provide greater consistency across institutional settings.

Formal Curriculum Comparisons Across Institutions. In their study of differential coursework patterns, Ratcliff and others (1990) utilized catalogues as one type of data source in their study of the relationships between formal and informal curricula at four institutions. Because they looked at college catalogues over time (on average, over five-year periods), they were able to chart the evolution of the formal curriculum, including additions and deletions of courses, development of majors, and specificity of general education requirements within and across institutions. One aspect of the catalogue study was an attempt to use class descriptions to determine if courses had gone through substantial revision, if they were equivalent to courses appearing in previous catalogues under different course numbers, different departments, or both, or if they were cross-listed with courses in other departments. Ratcliff and his colleagues found this process time-consuming and unreliable due to the inconsistencies in wording, use of terms, and content of class descriptions. At all four of the sample institutions, the research team also had difficulty in identifying the recommended versus required courses for meeting general education core requirements of various degree programs because of the way in which information was presented in the catalogues and the consistency with which the information was presented across catalogue sections. This disparity confounded data collection processes and forced the researchers to interpret words or phrases in course titles or descriptions in order to categorize responses. There were also questions about the comparability and degree of revision of courses whose descriptions did not change but whose course numbers were altered from year to year. The inconsistency in the kind and substance of information provided through college catalogues also hampered intra- and interinstitutional course comparisons as well as general education program comparisons.

The catalogue portion of Ratcliff and others' (1990) differential coursework patterns study offered important findings about general education curricula as well as confirmation of several results from previous studies. For instance, at each of the four institutions in the study, departments that had substantial course additions to the college catalogue were the same departments that experienced the greatest net curriculum change overall, whether in the form of different course numbers or titles, requirements or recommended courses, or additions or deletions of classes. The range of cumulative change in the formal curriculum across these four academic settings over the five-year study periods is noteworthy. At the lower end of change, institutions experienced around 14 percent cumulative change in the curriculum, and, at the high end, almost 20 percent. Given the vastness of college curricula, these two figures seem to indicate only minimal change. Yet, this change was in the general education component, and there continue to be significant constraints on course taking as a result of required and prerequisite coursework. Therefore, it seems these changes warrant closer examination to verify the forces driving the curriculum. Certainly, the degree of modification suggests that a generation of students might be involved in quite different general education experiences, in part due to changes in courses. Again, the impetus for and substantive nature of these curriculum changes and their effect on actual course taking are not apparent from catalogue data.

Utility of Catalogue Studies

From a review of studies using catalogues as primary data sources, we can critically examine the utility and limitations of this method of institutional-structural curriculum research. Individually, the studies add to our understanding of curriculum change in very specific arenas. By studying only catalogue data (the formal curriculum), we can discover growth or diminution of programs and disciplines, addition or deletion of numbers of courses in the overall curriculum, distribution of courses across curriculum components, course requirements, course prerequisites, and similar aspects that rely on strictly quantifiable data. As a result of such data gathering, we can describe the implicit assumptions of the curriculum and academic priorities at the institutional, school, departmental, and program levels. Catalogue studies provide important insights into objective, easily accessible, public proclamations of curriculum intent. To this end, they can provide useful information about the formal curriculum.

What also emerges consistently from all of the studies reviewed in this chapter are the difficulties inherent to catalogue research. For instance, what appear to be straightforward statements of curriculum goals are articulated in mission statements, course requirements, and so on. In following the implementation of mission statements and course requirements from the institution level to the program level, however, we find that the goals become ideals as schools and programs incorporate exceptions and unique requirements. Catalogue data reveal wide variation in the actual departmental expectations of what appeared to be institutionally consistent academic goals and objectives. Ambiguity in course titles and offerings, disparity in requirements, and flexibility in prerequisites across institutional levels are just some of the other issues facing catalogue researchers. There is also minimal explanation or elaboration of the rationale for course requirements or course sequencing at the institutional and program levels. The lack of continuity and rationale confounds the data gathering process and hinders the effort to draw accurate conclusions from catalogue data alone.

From a review of methodologies used in these catalogue studies, we gain insight into the strengths and weaknesses of this approach to curriculum research. Common research designs were used in the studies discussed above, with the exception of the work by Ratcliff and others (1990). Generally, the studies used predetermined categories of courses established de novo or derived from the work of previous scholars. Simple word counts or qualitative content analyses of course titles and descriptions were used to determine placement within each category, although there was no evidence that formal procedures were used to examine the content or concurrent validity of the categories. Nor was there sufficient documentation of tests for interrater reliability when teams of researchers were used for data collection and category assignment. Ambiguities and inconsistencies in wording make it difficult to assign courses to predetermined categories or to identify comparable programs, thus making subjective placement more likely and cross-unit comparisons problematic. Since for administrators and researchers a major attraction of using catalogues as primary data sources is their objectivity and accessibility, it is important to recognize the researcher subjectivity inherent to the collection and analysis of catalogue information. This is not to say that quantitative analysis is impossible or wholly unreliable. Rather, administrators and faculty should be aware that the process is time-consuming, that it captures only artifacts of curriculum philosophy and intent, and that it is far more arbitrary than is at first apparent.

What is clear from the review of the catalogue studies is that examination of curriculum change is enhanced by multiple data sources. Multiple sources of data are especially important when we look for the relationships between the curriculum intent (catalogue data) and outcomes (student course-taking behavior). The use of multiple data sources may simply involve the inclusion of various sections of a college catalogue, for example, mission statements and course descriptions in addition to course titles and degree requirements. By increasing the institutional sample size or using catalogues from several academic years, we can better study breadth and depth curriculum issues; the larger sample can mitigate certain methodological concerns, especially those related to statistical analyses, but it is likely to raise other issues such as a likely increase in catalogue discrepancies. Use of other quantitative data sources such as student transcripts or course syllabi can provide additional information, as can the use of qualitative data gathered through observations of classroom settings or through interviews of faculty and students about the meaning and purpose of coursework.

As a brief illustration of the way in which multiple data sources can enhance catalogue data in curriculum studies, we need only consider that the use of student transcripts strengthens conclusions drawn from catalogue data because the transcripts provide a basis for comparison between institutionally intended curriculum and actual student enactment of the curriculum. Transcripts can demonstrate the evolution of programs and curriculum intent in a different manner from catalogues in that actual student course taking can be evaluated. This analysis may reveal approved course requirement substitutions, new courses or one-time offerings, and titles of seminars or advanced course offerings that share a course number but reflect different content, all of which may not be reflected in the catalogue but may be important to understanding the full intellectual impact of the undergraduate curriculum. In an unobtrusive manner, we are able to gather additional information about the meaning that faculty ascribe to curriculum components by examining student transcripts as well. There is the assumption of some level of advising inherent to student course taking (what an individual adviser requires or allows as substitutions), as well as the faculty experimentation and curriculum development found in single-course offerings or advanced topical seminars that may not be found in the catalogue but can be noted on student transcripts. Because of their revelations regarding the actual curriculum, student transcripts are often seen as viable, sole sources of data for curriculum studies. Yet, even with the insights provided by transcript analyses, it is clear that a careful reading of the catalogue should still be pursued to identify prerequisites and courses required or recommended within and outside a field of study, all of which affect course-taking behavior but may not be easily differentiated when transcripts alone are used.

Implications of Catalogue Studies

College catalogues capture a curriculum moment in time. Within limits, they may also demonstrate change over time. What are missing in institutional-structural studies and what cannot be obtained from catalogue data alone are the process of or motivation for curriculum change and the true meaning of the curriculum for faculty and students. Despite elements of predictability and repetition, most faculty would agree that the college curriculum is intended to be a dynamic rather than a static entity, at least as experienced by the student and interpreted by the instructor-adviser. This dynamism is lost when we rely on a printed document as a primary data source, especially in the case of institutions where catalogues are reprinted (and therefore updated) on cycles of two or more academic years. The catalogues allow for certain assessments of the formal curriculum, yet as Veysey (1973) says, mere tinkering with the structure (as measured through catalogue studies) will have little impact on the quality of the curriculum because it never gets at the substance or the meaning of the informal curriculum. When we know only that general education requirements constitute fifty credits of the undergraduate curriculum, we know little about which classes actually are taken by students or the effectiveness of those credits in accomplishing the goals of general education; nor do we have much of a starting point for improving our education processes and outcomes.

Examples from the catalogue studies of the limitations of this approach and its ability to fully answer curriculum questions are many. For instance, we can determine, fairly confidently, the volume of courses in a given catalogue at several institutional levels. In finding a wide array of courses and course options, we might decide that this is a positive situation for students, from a cognitive or philosophical perspective. We may conclude that the degree of latitude in fulfilling academic requirements implies an institutional perspective on and value of student experimentation (Veysey, 1973). Yet, from catalogue data alone, we are really unable to ascertain the meaning behind the variation, latitude, and curriculum change. As opposed to a manifestation of institutional philosophy, substantial course offerings may simply be a result of faculty not appropriately updating the catalogue to reflect current practice. Using catalogue data in isolation, we are also unable to tie the formal curriculum to the course-taking behavior of students, leaving many questions related to latitude and flexibility unanswered. As an example, given a broad array of courses from which to choose, do students capitalize on experimentation, choosing "wisely" among opportunities for growth and knowledge expansion? When provided with upper- and lower-division courses that can fulfill similar requirements, do students make course decisions based on intellectual growth and development? What does it mean to the student to make a wise "learning use" of an elective course (Ratcliff and others, 1990)?

Those who have used catalogues as primary sources of data have shown that it is possible to demonstrate change in the college curriculum over time, whether at the program or institutional level. Again, what are less clear from the college catalogues are the logic behind the changes and the impact on institutional curriculum outcomes for students. If the general education curriculum undergoes a 20 percent change every five years, and that change appears substantive, as noted on average by Ratcliff and others (1990), how common are the learning experiences of students as they fulfill general education requirements? With that degree of change, what is indicated about the coherence and continuity of curriculum goals and philosophies at any level of the institution? It is easy to surmise that curriculum flexibility and change results in greater disparity between institutionally intended curriculum outcomes and student course-taking behavior. Without a complement of data sources, we are left only with supposition and no useful conclusions.

Catalogues provide verification of the formal curriculum for the generic student at a particular college or university. They are unlikely to present courses of study that are useful to students across ability levels. Ratcliff and others (1990) showed that certain courses were appropriate for students of lower ability in terms of knowledge gains, yet no distinctions were made in the college catalogues of the four sample institutions that reflected these ability differences. As a proposition for the future, it might be possible to link student assessment and transcript analysis to a recommended array of possible coursework associated with learning gains for different student populations, set out as part of the formal curriculum in the college catalogue. In this way, the catalogue becomes more of a living document than a sourcebook that seems outdated as soon as it is printed.

College catalogues can provide information useful to the study of curriculum. They present momentary reflections of curriculum ideals that may or may not be realized in student course taking and evidenced in faculty perceptions of the content of their courses. Catalogues, as public documents, present a snapshot of an institution's curriculum perspectives at a given point in time, perspectives that are open to multiple levels of interpretation as one moves from institutional rhetoric to individual adviser practice, to actual student enrollment. Catalogues are an important resource for understanding college curricula and, at least in their present format, are most effectively used in conjunction with other approaches to data collection.

References

Astin, A. W. "The Methodology of Research on College Impact, Part 1." *Sociology of Education,* 1970, *43,* 223–254.

Astin, A. W. *Four Critical Years: Effects of College on Beliefs, Attitudes, and Knowledge.* San Francisco: Jossey-Bass, 1977.

Becan-McBride, K. "Status of Requirements for Medical Technology Curricula." Paper presented at the annual meeting of the American Society of Medical Technology, May 1990. (ED 197 657)

Bergquist, W. H., Gould, R. A., and Greenberg, E. M. *Designing Undergraduate Education: A Systematic Guide.* San Francisco: Jossey-Bass, 1981.

Biglan, A. "The Characteristics of Subject Matter in Different Academic Areas." *Journal of Applied Psychology,* 1973, 57 (3), 195–203.

Blackburn, R., and others. *Changing Practice in Undergraduate Education.* Berkeley, Calif.: Carnegie Council for Policy Studies in Higher Education, 1976.

Boysen, A. R. "Technical Communications Curriculum for Undergraduate Colleges of Engineering: An Institutional Analysis Based upon Selected College Catalogues for the 1973–1974 Academic Year." *Dissertation Abstracts International,* 1979, *40,* 1236A.

Conrad, C. F. *The Undergraduate Curriculum: A Guide to Innovation and Reform.* Boulder, Colo.: Westview Press, 1978.

Dressel, P. L., and DeLisle, F. H. *Undergraduate Curriculum Trends.* Washington, D.C.: American Council on Education, 1969.

Fosdick, H. "Trends in Information Science Education." *Special Libraries,* 1984, 75 (4), 292–302.

Gillespie, P. P., and Cameron, K. M. "The Teaching of Acting in American Colleges and Universities, 1920–1960." *Communication Education,* 1986, 35 (4), 362–371.

Grace, J. D. "The Professionalization of Higher Education." Paper presented at the annual meeting of the American Educational Research Association, Chicago, April 1985. (ED 261 619).

Hefferlin, J.B.L. *Dynamics of Academic Reform.* San Francisco: Jossey-Bass, 1969.

Hurtado, S., Astin, A. W., and Dey, E. L. "Varieties of General Education Programs: An Empirically Based Taxonomy." *Journal of General Education,* 1991, *40,* 133–162.

Levine, A. *Handbook on Undergraduate Curriculum: Prepared for the Carnegie Council on Policy Studies in Higher Education.* San Francisco: Jossey-Bass, 1978.

LoGuidice, T. "Global and International Education at Lutheran-Sponsored and Affiliated Colleges: A Look at What Is and What Should Be." Paper presented at the annual meeting of the Association of Lutheran Faculties, October 1983. (ED 252 134)

McKeachie, W. J., Pintrich, P. R., Lin, Y. G., and Smith, D.A.F. *Teaching and Learning Strategies: A Review of the Research Literature.* Ann Arbor: National Center for Research to Improve Postsecondary Teaching and Learning, University of Michigan, 1986.

National Center for Education Statistics. *A Classification of Secondary School Courses.* Project summary report. Arlington, Va.: Evaluation Technologies, 1982. (ED 225 304)

Pascarella, E. T. "College Environmental Influences on Learning and Cognitive Development: A Critical Review and Synthesis." In J. Smart (ed.), *Higher Education: Handbook of Theory and Research.* Vol. 1. New York: Agathon, 1985.

Ratcliff, J. L., and others. *Development and Testing of a Cluster-Analytic Model for Identifying Coursework Patterns Associated with General Learned Abilities of College Students: Final Project Report.* Contract No. OERI-R-86-0016. University Park: Center for the Study of Higher Education, Pennsylvania State University, 1990.

Tenopir, C. "Information Science Education in the United States: Characteristics and Curricula." *Education for Information,* 1985, 3 (1), 3–28.

Toombs, W., Fairweather, J. S., Chen, A., and Amey, M. J. *Open to View: Practice and Purpose in General Education, 1988.* Final Report to the Exxon Education Foundation. University Park: Center for the Study of Higher Education, Pennsylvania State University, 1989.

Veysey, L. "Stability and Experience in the American Undergraduate Curriculum." In C. Keysen (ed.), *Content and Context: Essays on College Education.* New York: McGraw-Hill, 1973.

Waggaman, J. S. *Surrogate Learning Measures: Credit, Other Units, and Noncredit.* Tallahassee: Florida State Department of Education, Florida State University, 1980.

MARILYN J. AMEY is assistant professor of higher education at the University of Kansas, Lawrence. She has recently published articles on leadership in community colleges, faculty promotion and tenure, and administrative career expectations.

The Coursework Cluster Analysis Model provides insights regarding the most appropriate general education curriculum for students with different levels of abilities.

Is a Core Curriculum Best for Everybody?

Elizabeth A. Jones

Most American colleges and universities require students to study and complete a general education component in their undergraduate degree programs. Over one-third (37 percent) of the total curriculum is usually devoted to general education (Toombs, Fairweather, Chen, and Amey, 1989). This is a significant part of the curriculum. However, we do not know whether a core curriculum or a distribution requirement is most appropriate for enhancement of student learning.

The general education component often consists of institutionwide requirements designed to ensure that all students build skills for advanced study and lifelong learning. It is often designed to integrate learning in ways that broaden the student's understanding and ability to think about large and complex issues. Faculty make important decisions about how to structure general education and which courses should be included. They use a variety of approaches, ranging from a core curriculum to a set of distribution requirements. However, the questions of what students should learn in general education and how that curriculum should be organized remain open to debate.

The advocates for a core curriculum believe that all students benefit from taking the same courses, and that an educated person can be defined by a single set of prescribed courses (Boyer and Kaplan, 1977; National Endowment for the Humanities, 1984; Committee on Redefining the Meaning and Purpose of Baccalaureate Degrees, 1986). This view holds that all students benefit from a common set of required learning experiences. The underlying intent of the core curriculum is to overcome the fragmentation of knowledge that occurs from distribution schemes and to promote a general education program that is more coherent than a series of courses designed as introductions to various disciplines (Adelman, 1984).

There are many different conceptions regarding what content is most important for students to study. Boyer and Levine (1981) believe that all students should study a common body of knowledge: use of symbols, membership in groups and institutions, production and consumption activities in the world of work, relationships with nature, sense of time, and an understanding of values and beliefs. Cheney (1989) developed a different proposal but, in essence, still recommended that fifty hours be devoted to a common body of knowledge across several specific subject areas: one semester on the origins of civilization, one year on Western civilization, one semester on American civilization, two one-semester courses on other civilizations, two years of foreign language, one year of mathematics, one year of laboratory science, and one year of social science. Bloom (1987) stressed that the only major solution to the issues pertaining to the content of general education was to require the Great Books approach, where all students read certain classic texts. From the standpoint of these individuals, all students benefit by studying the same coursework.

The advocates for a distribution requirement believe that students should have choices regarding which courses best meet their own interests and abilities. The goal of the distribution requirement is to ensure that each student has some exposure to the content, traditions, and methods of the main subject fields (usually the humanities, social sciences, natural sciences, and, sometimes, the creative or performing arts). A distribution requirement gives students the opportunity to explore several different fields before selecting their majors. It allows students to select from a range of courses to satisfy an institution's general education goals. Advocates of this approach argue that there are many different types of students with varied backgrounds, interests, levels of preparation, and career aspirations who attend college (Hall and Kevies, 1982). Therefore, it is impossible to build a general education program on a common foundation; rather, there are multiple roads or paths to prepare students to become adult citizens in our diverse society.

The current debate over what students should learn and how it should be organized results from a dissatisfaction with student learning. Employers, policy makers, and faculty believe that students do not possess the necessary skills, abilities, knowledge, and personal qualities that are generally accepted as the characteristics of an educated person (Gaff, 1991). A number of reports have attempted to define those characteristics and to identify the subjects that help students to achieve them (Association of American Colleges, 1988; Study Group on the Conditions of Excellence in American Higher Education, 1984; National Endowment for the Humanities, 1984). The Association of American Colleges (1988, p. 3) broadly defined general education as "the cultivation of the knowledge, skills, and attitudes that all of us use and live by during most of our lives—whether as parents, citizens, lovers, travelers, participants in the arts, leaders, volunteers, or good samaritans." These reports served as important mechanisms to promote a national conversation about issues critical to general education. However, this dialogue did not lead colleges and universities to modify the curriculum, and thus little change in student performance was observed (Eaton, 1991). Therefore, faculty continue to debate and search for the best general education program to improve student learning.

Some of these reports (Carnegie Foundation for the Advancement of Teaching, 1977; Boyer and Levine, 1981) conclude that general education is a "disaster area" where there is no coherence, cohesion, or rationale for the programs. The Carnegie Foundation for the Advancement of Teaching (1977, p. 164) characterized general education as "an idea in distress" and noted that despite its central importance in the American college, it is "so exasperatingly beyond the reach of general consensus and understanding." Over a decade later, there is little evidence to suggest that the curriculum has more cohesion, clearer purpose, or greater effect on student learning (Eaton, 1991; Astin, 1991).

Today, policy makers, employers, and other constituencies continue to be dissatisfied with the level of students' abilities and skills developed during their undergraduate education. The National Governors' Association (1991) called for college graduates to increase substantially their skills to think critically, communicate effectively, and solve problems. Does a core curriculum provide the best learning experiences for students to acquire these necessary skills and abilities? Is the distribution requirement a solution to improve student learning and address the critics' complaints? Numerous reports and the public call upon institutions to improve the quality of the curriculum in order to enhance student learning.

Two major attempts have been made to measure student course selection in higher education. Zemsky (1989) analyzed over twenty-five thousand student transcripts and found that undergraduate work in the natural sciences and mathematics was quite limited and that the humanities were lacking in sequenced learning. He concluded that "there is a notable absence of structure and coherence in the college and university curricula. Our analyses indicate a continued fragmentation of an educational experience that ought to be greater than the sum of its parts" (1989, p. 7). Cheney (1989) analyzed humanities enrollments in colleges and universities. She discovered that in 1988–1989, it was possible for students to earn a bachelor's degree from 37 percent of the nation's higher education institutions without taking any course in history, 45 percent without taking an American or English literature course, 62 percent without taking a course in philosophy, and 77 percent without studying a foreign language (1989, p. 5). These two formal analyses supported many of the critics' assertions outlined in various reports.

There continues to be a large difference of opinion about what the specific goals for general education should be and what sequences of coursework help students to attain those goals. Different institutions have different missions and have therefore developed different conceptions of what constitutes a general education program. But these differences should not be permitted to inhibit or delay institutions' efforts to explore the effectiveness of their general education programs.

Challenges for the Assessment of General Education

The assessment of general education is critical in order to improve student learning and strengthen general education. However, faculty leaders face many challenges in their assessment efforts. There are different conceptions of general education. Colleges and universities have defined different goals and objectives for general education. They also structure the curriculum in different ways. Some institutions have adopted a core curriculum to achieve their goals, while others have implemented a distribution requirement. There also has not been a clear way to link students' learning to the courses that they take. These differences make it difficult to determine whether a core curriculum or a distribution requirement helps students to improve their learning and attain an institution's curriculum goals. Quality assessments of student learning in general education can help provide answers.

Many faculty and administrators who are committed to quality improvement encourage the monitoring and evaluation of institutional performance relative to student learning. Eighty percent of the nation's postsecondary institutions have reported using outcomes assessment activities to evaluate program quality and educational effectiveness (El-Khawas, 1989). However, most institutions are in the beginning stages of planning and designing assessment activities. The American Council on Education (1991) reported that only 30 percent of the nation's two- and four-year colleges and universities operate comprehensive student assessment programs; an additional 60 percent reported that they planned to establish such programs in the future. At the same time, most institutions are attempting to reform general education (Gaff, 1991). Rarely have assessment initiatives and curriculum reform efforts informed one another. While the evidence suggests that most colleges and universities are trying to improve student learning, the results of their efforts have yet to materialize (Astin, 1991; Eaton, 1991). Why has so much effort led to so few results?

In many institutions, general education and assessment go forward on separate paths, in different parts of the institution, often with the responsibility for overseeing the activities given to different committees with different interests (Hutchings, Marchese, and Wright, 1991). These are major shortcomings of reform efforts that result from the lack of a clear way to tie student assessment to curriculum reform.

General education programs often lack "concrete goals or outcomes statements and students move through the program in who-knows-how-many permutations and configurations" (Hutchings, Marchese, and Wright, 1991, p. 6). These programs involve almost all departments and most faculty members. Yet few faculty have devoted time to the assessment of general education. Often general education has been mandated by either administrators or by other constituencies. A change in one part of the program affects units and individuals involved in other parts. It is a challenge to get the faculty as a whole to take responsibility for general education. It is even difficult for the college community to reach a consensus among its constituents on the goals of general education, how to structure it, or the best measures to use in the assessment of general learned abilities.

Many institutions are dissatisfied with their assessment results and the methods used to gather and analyze information (American Council on Education, 1991). Faculty and administrators need to establish stronger links between what students study in college and what they learn. The Coursework Cluster Analysis Model (CCAM) described by Ratcliff (this volume, Chapter One) provides academic leaders with a way to make a more meaningful connection between undergraduate curriculum content and improved student learning. In addition, the model also provides answers to the question of whether a core curriculum or a set of distribution requirements best improves student learning.

Insights from the Coursework Cluster Analysis Model

The undergraduate curriculum is a complex, interwoven fabric consisting of a large and broad array of coursework. The average undergraduate student selects thirty-five to forty-five courses to fulfill the baccalaureate requirements from the list of eight hundred to five thousand courses offered at colleges and universities. From this multitude of courses, faculty have designated certain courses to provide the foundation for the general education program. The substance and the structure of the program articulate for students and other constituents the academic purposes, policies, and goals of the institution. Faculty believe that through student selection from the approved array of courses, certain types of learning most important to the institution are achieved.

In order to determine if certain types of learning were being achieved by students, James Ratcliff and I used several measures of general learning and the transcripts of graduating seniors at five different types of institutions. Through application of the CCAM, we identified the coursework taken by students who showed large gains on the measures of general learning. For example, a measure of analytical reasoning was used to assess students' ability to understand a structure of relationships and to deduce new information from these relationships. This measure is related to the Watson-Glaser and Cornell Critical Thinking tests. The CCAM identifies the sequences of courses that help students to improve their learning. This information is particularly useful in efforts to strengthen student learning in critical thinking, which is one of the national education goals (National Governors' Association, 1991).

We found that different patterns of coursework rather than single, specific courses produce different types of gains in learning (Jones and Ratcliff, 1990; Ratcliff, 1988; Ratcliff and Jones, 1990). For example, course sequences in a variety of disciplines such as mathematics, economics, music, physical therapy, and business were associated with student improvement in mathematics. Course sequences in English, literature, writing, accounting, finance, and marketing were associated with student gains in reading comprehension. For analytical reasoning, course sequences in logic, statistics, philosophy, chemistry, economics, history, psychology, and political science enhanced student learning. The results demonstrate that there are many courses that strengthen student learning. That is, contrary to traditional notions, English and literature courses are not the only areas that contribute to student gains in reading comprehension; likewise, mathematics and statistics are not the only courses that contribute to student improvement in mathematics.

In examining our results, we looked at two different levels of student abilities. One group consisted of students with high abilities, and the second group consisted of students with low abilities relative to the norms of a particular institution. We found differences in the learning of these two groups. We sought to determine if the views of the core curriculum advocates or those of the distribution requirement advocates more fully explained the extent of general education coursework associated with gains in the general learned abilities between the two groups of students. If all university students benefit from a core curriculum (a single set of general education coursework), then the same courses should improve student learning in both high- and low-ability groups.

We found that different sets of courses helped students of different ability levels to improve. For example, low-ability students at the institutions examined did not complete the science sequences offered as part of the general education sequence. The curriculum package of Chemistry 101, 102, and 103 (including organic and inorganic) provided students with the main concepts, terms, and theories of the discipline. This course sequence was designed to produce a degree of learning that would, ideally, help students attain the institutions' general education goals. High-ability students selected and completed the sequence to fulfill part of their general education requirements. However, low-ability students took only Chemistry 101 and then received either a low or failing grade. Next, they enrolled in other science courses such as physics or biology and had a similar negative experience. Although these low-ability students eventually satisfied the general education requirements, they repeatedly encountered negative educational experiences because the curriculum was set at and their fellow, high-ability students were performing at a level exceeding their own abilities. Furthermore, while high-ability students completed the planned course patterns in chemistry, low-ability students completed only single courses in this and other science sequences.

We found that students who showed gains in the high-ability group did not take the same coursework as those who gained in the low-ability group. In the majority of cases, coursework selected by high-ability students led to gains in their learning, whereas for the majority of low-ability students the coursework selected did not lead to gains in learning. However, we were able to identify discrete sets of courses that were beneficial to low-ability students.

Our findings argue against the establishment of a core curriculum. The results from our work support the view of advocates for a distribution requirement, since students who showed improvement in the high-ability group did not take the same coursework as students in the low-ability group. Our findings, however, do not argue for a wide range of options in a distributional general education requirement. Instead, they suggest that discrete arrays of coursework are more appropriate and productive, as tailored for different ability levels of students. Prerequisites and specific course sequences should be designed to promote the cumulative development of general learned abilities. The example discussed above demonstrates that we can do more for those students who are among the lower ranges of abilities relative to other students at the same institution. We need to reform our general education requirements so that they take into account the differences in student abilities, interests, and levels of preparation. Today's students exhibit a greater diversity in their talents and career aspirations. Our work does not support the view that the same courses for all students lead to productive gains in their learning and achievement of general education goals.

Through the identification of clusters of coursework associated with improvements in student learning, faculty have information to evaluate the general education component of their curriculum. Faculty know which courses consistently contribute over time to the improvement of student learning. Courses outside the general education requirements can become candidates for inclusion in the curriculum. Courses in the general education sequence that are not found to be associated with improvement in student learning can be revised, enhanced, or deleted from the curriculum.

Institutions have an obligation to educate the students whom they admit. This obligation includes low-ability students. The extent to which general education courses affect the learning of both high- and low-ability students is relevant to decisions about how wide-ranging the distributional options should be given the education goals of each institution.

A prescribed core curriculum and an entirely free choice of elective courses were not supported by our work. However, clear sequences and combinations of different coursework were found to have distinct and different benefits for high-ability and low-ability students. Also, we found that general education goals are not achieved only through lower-division courses. Upper-division courses in a variety of areas contribute strongly to the development of general learned abilities. This challenges the traditional notion that only lower-division general education coursework is productive for students when completed during the freshmen and sophomore years.

Unfortunately, the college curriculum is often characterized as a fragmented entity that "has been likened to a smorgasbord, or a spare room filled with a miscellany of castoffs" (Gaff, 1991, p. 21). If we can identify effective course sequences for different ability levels of students, then we can strive toward creating greater coherence and cohesion in general education.

Conclusion

During the 1980s, the critics of general education complained about students' abilities and skills developed during their undergraduate education. Critics emphasized the inability of faculty, committees, and the academic leadership to effectively define the content and structure of general education. They also stressed the lack of clarity of general education goals despite the long-time discussion of this topic. The critics noted the difficulty in establishing effective general education programs due to the absence of clearly identified faculty charged with oversight of these programs and the lack of administrative support.

The debates regarding the content and structure of general education continue today. It is not easy to resolve the tensions surrounding fundamental decisions about curriculum content since they reflect diverse institutional values and missions. Some faculty are reluctant to commit to a clearly defined approach to general education for fear that the program will be found deficient. However, if we wait for the perfect general education program to emerge, then we make little progress toward articulating clearer education goals and may ultimately neglect to move student learning to a higher level.

Through use of the CCAM, administrators and faculty can begin to gain a better understanding of which particular sequences of courses improve student learning and which courses help students attain particular general education goals. In our research, we found that a core curriculum is not appropriate for college students today. Students with different abilities benefit from different sets of coursework. A specific and highly limited set of courses will not improve all student learning. Instead, the curriculum can be designed to provide those learning experiences that are related to different levels of student abilities.

It is helpful to gain information about student learning in general education programs, even if these programs possess some flaws. With information about student learning, its links to coursework and education goals, we can begin to determine the strengths and weaknesses of general education programs, the kind of substantive information needed to improve general education's content and structure. A distribution plan for general education can be identified that matches students' particular interests and abilities. Such a distribution plan with arrays of coursework is necessary since students are entering college with diverse backgrounds and levels of preparation.

The CCAM can be used to identify effective course sequences for different ability levels of students. We can then strive to overcome the fragmentation associated with general education and improve the undergraduate curriculum to enhance the learning of a diverse group of students.

References

Adelman, C. *Starting with Students*. Washington, D.C.: National Institute of Education, 1984.

American Council on Education. *Assessing Assessment*. Washington, D.C.: American Council on Education, 1991.

Association of American Colleges. *A New Vitality in General Education*. Washington, D.C.: Association of American Colleges, 1988.

Astin, A. W. *Assessment for Excellence: The Philosophy and Practice of Assessment and Evaluation in Higher Education*. New York: Macmillan, 1991.

Bloom, A. *Closing of the American Mind*. New York: Simon & Schuster, 1987.

Boyer, E. L., and Kaplan, M. *Educating for Survival*. New Rochelle, N.Y.: Change Magazine Press, 1977.

Boyer, E. L., and Levine, A. *A Quest for Common Learning*. Washington, D.C.: Carnegie Foundation for the Advancement of Teaching, 1981.

Carnegie Foundation for the Advancement of Teaching. *Missions of the College Curriculum: A Contemporary View with Suggestions*. San Francisco: Jossey-Bass, 1977.

Cheney, L. V. *50 Hours: A Core Curriculum for College Students*. Washington, D.C.: National Endowment for the Humanities, 1989.

Committee on Redefining the Meaning and Purpose of Baccalaureate Degrees. Association of American Colleges. *Integrity in the College Curriculum: A Report to the Academic Community*. Washington, D.C.: Association of American Colleges, 1985.

Eaton, J. S. *The Unfinished Agenda: Higher Education and the 1980s*. New York: Macmillan, 1991.

El-Khawas, E. *1989 Campus Trends Survey*. Washington, D.C.: American Council on Education, 1989.

Gaff, J. G. *New Life for the College Curriculum: Assessing Achievements and Furthering Progress in the Reform of General Education*. San Francisco: Jossey-Bass, 1991.

Hall, J., and Kevies, B. (eds.). *In Opposition to Core Curriculum: Alternative Models for Undergraduate Education*. Westport, Conn.: Greenwood, 1982.

Hutchings, P., Marchese, T., and Wright, B. *Using Assessment to Strengthen General Education*. Washington, D.C.: American Association for Higher Education, 1991.

Jones, E. A., and Ratcliff, J. L. "Effective Coursework Patterns and Faculty Perceptions of the Development of General Learned Abilities." Paper presented at the annual meeting of the Association for the Study of Higher Education, Portland, Oregon, November 1990.

National Endowment for the Humanities. *To Reclaim a Legacy: A Report on the Humanities in Higher Education.* Washington, D.C.: National Endowment for the Humanities, 1984.

National Governors' Association. *Redefining the Possible: Achieving the National Education Goals.* Washington, D.C.: National Governors' Association, 1991.

Ratcliff, J. L. "The Development of a Cluster Analytic Model for Determining the Associated Effects of Coursework Patterns on Student Learning." Paper presented at the annual meeting of the American Educational Research Association, New Orleans, April 1988.

Ratcliff, J. L., and Jones, E. A. "General Learning at a Women's College." Paper presented at the annual meeting of the Association for the Study of Higher Education, Portland, Oregon, November 1990.

Study Group on the Conditions of Excellence in American Higher Education. National Institute of Education. *Involvement in Learning: Realizing the Potential of American Higher Education.* Washington, D.C.: Government Printing Office, 1984.

Toombs, W., Fairweather, J. S., Chen, A., and Amey, M. J. *Open to View: Practice and Purpose in General Education, 1988.* University Park: Center for the Study of Higher Education, Pennsylvania State University, 1989.

Zemsky, R. *Structure and Coherence: Measuring the Undergraduate Curriculum.* Washington, D.C.: Association of American Colleges, 1989.

ELIZABETH A. JONES is a research associate at Pennsylvania State University, University Park, where she directs a Fund for the Improvement of Postsecondary Education project that is designed to help the university develop an innovative assessment program for general education. She is also associate editor of the Journal of General Education.

Do community college courses with the same time and description as those offered by senior institutions really produce the same level of student learning?

Using Assessment as a Basis for the Articulation of Transfer Students

James L. Ratcliff

During the 1950s and 1960s, states built systems of public higher education designed to provide greater access to the masses. Community, junior, and technical colleges were major additions to these systems. Over half of the two-year colleges came into existence in the two decades following the passage of the Higher Education Act of 1965. In that year, there were 654 two-year colleges, representing less than one-third of all higher education institutions. By 1985, there were 1,350 two-year colleges constituting 40 percent of all institutions of higher education. In 1965, two-year colleges enrolled 24 percent of all first-time college freshmen; by 1985, they enrolled 44 percent of all freshmen students (Snyder, 1989).

These state systems of higher education were built on conflicting assumptions of equality and selectivity. For example, the California State Master Plan called for the top 12 percent of high school graduates to be admitted to the University of California system, the top one-third of high school graduates to be eligible for admission to the California State University system, and the balance of high school graduates to have access to the state system of community colleges. This plan allowed research universities, such as the University of California at Berkeley, to remain highly selective institutions and to maintain their leadership positions and reputations for excellence (Cohen and Brawer, 1989; Kintzer and Wattenbarger, 1986). Hence, the Master Plan implicitly underwrote the notion of institutional diversity and inequality.

At the same time, students completing associate degrees at the California community colleges can apply for admission to institutions within the University of California and California State University systems and, if accepted, transfer and apply their collegiate work completed at the community college toward a baccalaureate degree. The assumption underlying transfer is that work satisfactorily completed at one institution may be equivalent to that completed at another. Thus, while the Master Plan in California was built on a notion of selectivity and institutional diversity, there was also a presumption of the basic similarity, comparability, and equality of coursework completed at different institutions within the statewide system of higher education. Similar notions of institutional diversity, selectivity, and distinctiveness are found in other state systems of higher education in the United States (Clark, 1985).

The question remains, however, about the extent to which student learning achieved at one institution is really comparable to that expected at another. The assumption that similar courses offered by different institutions produce similar effects on student learning has rarely received empirical examination. Other chapters in this volume show ways in which assessment scores, faculty interviews, course syllabi, and examinations can be used to inform and guide the reform and revision of undergraduate curriculum, student advising, and faculty development. This chapter illustrates how the Coursework Cluster Analysis Model (CCAM) can be used to examine interinstitutional and statewide policies regarding articulation and transfer of student credits (for a description of the CCAM, see Ratcliff, this volume, Chapter One).

Studies of articulation and transfer have been primarily concerned with three separate issues: the transfer and acceptance of community college coursework toward the general education requirements of a baccalaureate-granting institution, the transfer and acceptance of credit toward major or minor fields of specialization of a baccalaureate-granting institution, and the transfer and acceptance of vocational and technical education credits earned at a community college as elective or specialization coursework at a baccalaureate-granting institution. The CCAM is designed to examine coursework and student outcomes assessment in institutions with distributional general education requirements; it is ideally suited to answer questions regarding the optimum match between learner and learning environment in situations where the student has a wide range of curriculum options. Thus, in this chapter, we are concerned with only one kind of articulation issue, that is, the efficacy of coursework taken at one institution in fulfilling the general education goals of the second (usually, baccalaureate-granting) institution.

Prior research on issues of articulation and transfer has focused on credit loss and time to attainment of the bachelor's degree. Also, there is a substantial body of literature on "transfer shock" and the success of transfer students in making the transition from community college to baccalaureate-granting institution. Rarely, however, has the examination extended to the long-term learning shown by transfer students. Studies have used cumulative grade point average (GPA), terms enrolled, and credits earned as measures of student progress, persistence, performance, and degree completion (Richardson and Doucette, 1980; Giddings, 1985).

Student outcomes assessments hold the promise of examining the relative learning gains of transfer and native students at a baccalaureate-granting institution. Given that baccalaureate-granting colleges and universities received transfer students from a wide variety of institutions, it is usually practical to limit such investigations to the two, three, or four geographically adjacent community colleges that typically account for the majority of transfer students at any given four-year institution.

Performance of Community College Students

Community colleges are relatively new institutions, and the viability of their transfer function rests on the acceptance of community college credits by baccalaureate-granting institutions. Consequently, a great deal of research on community college transfer students has been devoted to comparisons of their performance relative to native students, those who began their undergraduate studies at the institution granting their bachelor's degrees. Koos (1924), a pioneer researcher of the two-year college, studied the performance of ninety-five junior college graduates and seventy-five native graduates of the University of Wisconsin; he found no statistical difference in the mean GPAs of the two groups. De Ritter (1951) reviewed the literature on junior college student performance, concluding that transfer students performed as well or better than native students; although transfer students showed some decline in GPA at the time of transfer, their GPAs upon graduation were comparable to those of native students.

By 1965, differences between community college transfer student and native student performance began to emerge. In a national study, Knoell and Medsker (1965) compared community college transfer students with students who transferred from four-year colleges and with native students. GPAs of the transfer students were lower than their native counterparts. Transfer students had higher GPAs during their freshman and sophomore years, lower GPAs during their junior (transfer) year, and GPAs that approached but did not match those of native students in their senior year. Students who transferred after two years were more successful than those who transferred after only one year at the community college. Hills (1965) reviewed studies comparing transfer and native students. He found that twenty-two of thirty-three studies showed that native students performed better, seven studies showed no difference between the two groups, and four indicated that transfer students outperformed native students. By 1965, the performance of community college students relative to native counterparts was on the decline.

Thus, the parallel performance of community college students has not been sustained. As the number of community college students and institutions grew from 1965 to 1985, the relative performance, persistence, and degree attainment rates slipped (Kintzer and Wattenbarger, 1981). Part of this drop is attributable to the fact that community colleges were attracting a wider (and thereby lower) range of student abilities. After controlling for incoming ability of the students, Nickens (1972), Richardson and Doucette (1980), and Giddings (1985) found no significant differences between transfer and native student performance.

Adelman (1992, p. 16) noted that most studies of community college student ability or talent use single, aggregate measures, and few reveal what constitutes the score basis for defining high ability. He found that 80 percent of the students with high ability and high academic preparation for postsecondary education did not attend community colleges. He thus found the argument spurious that high-ability students from low socioeconomic backgrounds attend the community college and are dissuaded from earning bachelor's degrees (for example, Folger, Astin, and Bayer, 1970; Karabel, 1972; Brint and Karabel, 1989; Grubb, 1991). Adelman also noted that students in the National Longitudinal Study of 1972 who earned postsecondary degrees of any kind from any type of institution took college preparatory curricula in mathematics and science in high school.

Blame for the downward spiral in community college transfer student performance, persistence, and baccalaureate-degree attainment has been cast not only on the community colleges but also on the four-year colleges and universities. The community colleges are accused of diverting students from transfer to occupational curricula (Brint and Karabel, 1989), and of providing weak remedial, advisory, and academic programs (Grubb, 1991). Four-year colleges and universities are accused of "deteriorating articulation services for transfers (e.g., orientation, counseling, financial aid, and housing), the lack of community college/university communication regarding the mechanics of transferring courses and credits, competition from the universities for ethnic minorities underrepresented in higher education, the lack of uniformity in credit acceptance among the campuses of multiversities" (Kintzer and Wattenbarger, 1986, p. 1).

Articulation Practices and Assumptions About Course Comparability

Articulation plans are viewed by two- and four-year institutions as the primary vehicles for ensuring the success of community college transfer students. A question basic to most articulation plans is whether courses offered at one institution are really comparable to those at another. Kintzer and Wattenbarger (1986) described three broad types of articulation plans: (1) formal and legally based policies (for example, Florida and Illinois), (2) state system policies (for example, North Carolina and Washington), and

(3) voluntary agreements among individual institutions or systems (for example, California and Michigan). Each type of articulation arrangement, agreement, or policy relies on one of several mechanisms for facilitating transfer of credits.

One such mechanism is common course numbering. For example, since 1980, all public community colleges and universities in Florida have operated on a common calendar and course-numbering system. The Florida State Board of Education examines each new course proposed by an institution; if the course is deemed to be similar in content and level to another offered within the system, the course receives the same number. Students taking that course at a community college may then transfer the course credits to a public university with the assurance that it will be regarded as comparable to the course by the same number offered by the university. If a course is deemed to be unique within the curriculum offerings of Florida colleges and universities, it receives a unique course number.

A common course numbering scheme requires that all institutions within the system develop undergraduate coursework that is basically the same (for example, Chemistry 101: Organic Chemistry) at each institution. Thus, when students seek to move from one institution to another, it is presumed that they have had basically the same curriculum experience. For example, if Chemistry 101 is part of the baccalaureate general education requirements, then the Chemistry 101 transfer credits may be applied to fulfillment of those requirements. States such as Florida, Arizona, and Georgia have such systems. The assumption is that courses with the same number produce the same effect in terms of general student learning, regardless of institutional setting or background of the students enrolled.

A second articulation mechanism is the core curriculum. In Texas, the Coordinating Board directed that a basic core curriculum of general education courses be established in Texas community colleges that would be freely transferable to all public institutions of higher education in the state (Kintzer and Wattenbarger, 1986, p. 26). Here, the system or the state has established a uniform set of courses that all students must take. Again, the plan is based on the assumption that courses offered at one institution affect its students' learning in ways comparable to how courses with the same names at another institution affect that institution's students.

A third articulation mechanism is the course comparability catalogue. Where no statewide system of articulation exists, or where articulation is expressed in terms of credit hours rather than specific courses, senior-level colleges and universities develop lists of courses at specific community colleges that they will accept toward fulfillment of the general education requirements for their bachelor's degrees. For example, two two-credit courses in chemistry at the community college might be judged as comparable to a four-credit course in chemistry at the baccalaureate-granting institution. Course comparability catalogues, like core curricula and common course numbering, are based on the assumption of the sameness of effect of different courses offered in different institutional settings to students of diverse backgrounds. This assumption has yet to be fully tested.

The debate continues concerning the structure and content of general education (Committee on Redefining the Meaning and Purpose of Baccalaureate Degrees, 1985; Association of American Colleges, 1988; Study Group on the Conditions of Excellence in American Higher Education, 1984; National Endowment for the Humanities, 1984). Yet, evidence has emerged that different students experience different subenvironments within colleges and universities, particularly in relation to their formal coursework (Pascarella, 1985; Ratcliff, 1989; Jones and Ratcliff, 1990). At one end of the debate continuum, there are advocates for a core curriculum who believe that general education should consist of prescribed coursework required of all students (Boyer and Kaplan, 1977; National Endowment for the Humanities, 1984). They believe that one curriculum is appropriate and fits all students. At the other end, there are advocates of the distribution model, which consists of "requirements designed to ensure that each student takes a minimum number of courses or credits in specified academic areas" (Levine, 1978, p. 11). Students at many colleges meet distribution requirements by enrolling in courses selected from many offerings in different subject fields. The advocates of distribution requirements believe that different curricula are necessary for different students based on student interest and ability. Common course numbering and systemwide core curriculum requirements are based on the assumption that the effects of commonly named and labeled courses are the same.

A Trial Investigation of Course Comparability

In this chapter, the CCAM is used to examine student transcripts and test scores of native and transfer students at an urban state university to determine the extent to which general education coursework with comparable course numbering produces common effects in the general learning abilities of these college students. Given the views of the advocates of common course numbering systems as articulation mechanisms, the fundamental question here is whether the effect of coursework at a two-year college is comparable in its effect on general learned abilities to that of the identically numbered coursework at an urban doctorate-granting university (hereafter called Southern University) within the same state system of higher education. First, my colleagues and I established relationships between student coursework and common measures of general learned abilities, the Scholastic Aptitude Test (SAT) and the General Test of the Graduate Record Examination (GRE). Second, we examined if these relationships were the same for native students (those who began their education at Southern University) and for transfer students.

The study described here is an exploratory or trial investigation for a number of reasons. Ideally, a baccalaureate-granting institution would have a set of clearly articulated general education goals and a systematic program of student outcomes assessment to determine the extent to which the students and the institution are meeting those goals. Unfortunately, this ideal is not the case here or in most of higher education. General education goals and assessment criteria most often have been developed independently. But if a university had such a set of clearly expressed general education goals and a program of student assessment to determine the extent to which each student attained them, then it would be possible to evaluate the relative educational attainment of both transfer and native students. Goals for general education might include content learning, cognitive development, and the development of values and attitudes toward learning (Terenzini, 1989). With a clear set of general education goals and an assessment program to match, we could use the CCAM to identify coursework patterns of transfer and native students to determine if similar sets of courses were associated with attainment of the general education goals.

In the following study, there was a statewide definition of a core curriculum in general education, which was in reality a modified distribution requirement; that is, students were asked to assemble course credits in four broad areas rather than to enroll in specifically prescribed courses and course sequences. There were no clearly defined general education goals, nor was there a comprehensive assessment program at Southern University to determine the extent to which students were attaining those goals. Furthermore, beyond SAT scores and GRE scores, we had no measures of content learning or values and attitudes of students toward learning; in short, we had only broad assessment measures of general learned abilities. Consequently, we were able to answer the questions of course comparability and the efficacy of the statewide core only within the context of the development of general cognitive abilities of students and only in relation to one university and one two-year college in the system. Nevertheless, the investigation provides a blueprint for examining articulation policies across multiple institutions within a statewide system using multiple assessment criteria and student transcripts.

Sample. Two stratified samples of graduating seniors were drawn from the doctorate-granting university (Southern University). Since the size of each sample was small, the two were combined. Two subsamples were drawn from this combined sample. One subsample consisted of 76 students who had earned up to ninety quarter credits at a nearby public two-year college and had subsequently transferred to Southern University. The second subsample consisted of 168 native students who had earned their credits exclusively from Southern University. These students graduated from Southern during the 1986–1987 and 1987–1988 academic years. Analysis indicated that the sample was proportional to the distribution of SAT scores, majors, and socioeconomic characteristics of the population of graduating seniors at this institution.

There were 3,427 courses listed on the 76 transcripts of the students in the transfer group, indicating that, on average, each of these students had enrolled in 45.1 courses as part of the baccalaureate-degree program. There were 1,088 unduplicated courses on the transfer transcripts, in 177 of which five or more students had enrolled. These 177 courses were the subject of subsequent quantitative cluster analysis.

There were 7,850 courses listed on the 168 transcripts of the students in the native group, indicating that, on average, each of these students had enrolled in 46.7 courses as part of the baccalaureate-degree program. There were 1,244 unduplicated courses on the native transcripts, in 300 of which five or more students had enrolled. These 300 courses also were the objects of further analysis.

Differences Between Native and Transfer Students. There were differences between the native and transfer students in background and prior achievement. Gender is a factor related to academic performance. In our subsamples, 65.8 percent of the transfer group was female, and 56.5 percent of the native group was female. As Adelman (1992) and others have noted, women tend to enroll in community colleges in greater proportions than do men. Ethnicity is also related to academic performance. In the present study, 92 percent of the transfer group was white, while 35.1 percent of the native group was white. Major field of study has been shown to be correlated to student performance on the GRE. The distribution of majors in the transfer group was roughly the same as that in the native group. Majors in accounting, journalism, management, marketing, and psychology were frequent in both groups. One transfer student first enrolled in the community college in 1958, whereas two native students began their enrollment in 1970. Overall, 30.4 percent of the native students and 24.8 percent of the transfer students began their enrollment prior to 1980. These distributions corresponded to national distributions, with a higher proportion of transfer students enrolling on a part-time basis (Adelman, 1992; Grubb, 1991). Students in the transfer and native groups were clearly planning some form of postbaccalaureate study: 56.6 percent of the transfer students and 66.1 percent of the native students planned to work for a master's degree. Approximately 16 percent of the transfer and native students planned to enter a doctoral program. These students planned advanced study in greater proportion than most undergraduates (Adelman, 1992) and reflect the self-selected nature of the sample.

The educational attainment of parents has been shown to be positively correlated to student achievement in college. In the present study, 25 percent of the fathers and 15.8 percent of the mothers of the transfer group had attained a high school diploma or its equivalent, while over 14.3 percent of the fathers and 30.9 percent of the mothers of native students had attained a high school diploma. Only 1.3 percent of the fathers and the mothers of transfer students had attained at least a bachelor's degree, while 10.1 percent of the fathers and 9.5 percent of the mothers of native students had attained a bachelor's degree. Clearly, the native students came from families where greater proportions of the parents had higher levels of education. The transfer students had higher mean SAT scores (Verbal = 440, Math = 452) than those of the total population of Southern University students (Verbal = 396, Math = 414). The transfer group exceeded the native group in entering educational ability as well.

Contrary to popular conceptions of community college and university students, the Southern University transfer students were less likely to be from a racial or ethnic minority and were slightly less likely to be part-time students. While their parents had less formal education than did the parents of native students, the transfer group entered college with stronger academic abilities. For these reasons, results of this exploratory investigation should not be generalized to other community college or university populations. What is important to note, however, is that there were substantial differences in student background and achievement between the transfers and the natives.

Differences in Performance on the GRE. When the effect of the precollege learning (as measured by the SAT) was statistically removed, significant differences appeared in the residual scores of the native and the transfer groups. Table 4.1 displays the results of the regression analyses of individual GRE item-type scores on SAT subscores. For both the transfer and native groups, the greatest amount of variance in item-type residuals, including the greatest standard error and standard deviation, were found in analytical reasoning. Analytical reasoning is also the area in which the greatest gains in learning were evidenced in other student groups and institutions that we have studied (Ratcliff, 1989; Jones and Ratcliff, 1990). The variance in the residuals had implications for our cluster analysis. GRE item types with greater variance played a more significant role in the sorting of courses into clusters.

While the residual means describe the direction of change in general learned abilities (positive or negative), the standard deviations of residuals give estimates of the variation in change. The greatest variation in residuals occurred among the native group. The greatest variation for both groups occurred in the analytical reasoning item type. These data indicated differences in general learned abilities according to the entering SAT scores. Also, these data suggested that the effect of the undergraduate experience varied between the transfer group and the native group. Specifically, incoming ability as measured by the SAT accounted for less of the score variance among the transfer group. Using residuals as

Table 4.1. Summary of Regression Analyses of GRE Item Types on SAT Subscores for the Transfer and Native Groups of Southern University

Dependent Variables	Code	Transfer Group (N = 76)			Native Group (N = 168)		
		F	$p > F$	Adjusted R^2	F	$p > F$	Adjusted R^2
GRE item-type scores							
Sentence completion	SC	32.148	.0001	.2934	124.610	.0001	.4253
Analogies	ANA	35.046	.0001	.3122	93.910	.0001	.3575
Reading comprehension	RD	47.848	.0001	.3845	97.122	.0001	.3653
Antonyms	ANT	28.616	.0001	.2691	143.335	.0001	.4601
Quantitative comparisons	QC	42.137	.0001	.3542	182.350	.0001	.5206
Regular mathematics	RM	34.089	.0001	.3061	146.754	.0001	.4660
Data interpretation	DI	11.847	.0010	.1264	62.317	.0001	.2686
Analytical reasoning	ARE	28.346	.0001	.2672	99.616	.0001	.3713
Logical reasoning	LR	18.551	.0001	.1896	74.640	.0001	.3060
Raw SAT subscores							
Verbal	GRE	62.267	.0001	.4496	266.909	.0001	.6142
Quantitative	GRE	51.195	.0001	.4009	268.383	.0001	.6155
Analytical	GRE	37.490	.0001	.3273	143.057	.0001	.4596

Note: GRE = Graduate Record Examination and SAT = Scholastic Aptitude Test.

proxies for gains in general learned abilities, we found that the transfer students had greater gains than did native students in all nine areas measured by the GRE.

The students in the two groups did not register strong positive gains once the effect of their precollege SAT scores was removed. Nevertheless, some students gained and others declined in general learned ability within both groups. These cluster analyses differentiated between courses taken by students who showed gains on the item types and those who declined. While the sum of all residuals is zero, when residuals were aggregated by course, some courses had positive mean residuals while others had negative mean residuals for the students who enrolled in them. Courses with five or more students had slightly positive average mean course residuals, which indicated that the average Southern University student did select common coursework associated with gains in general learned abilities.

Based on the student residuals obtained from the regression analyses described above, the mean residuals for each course enrolling five or more students were calculated for all nine of the GRE item types. This procedure did not assume that the specific gains of the students enrolled in each course were directly caused by that course. Rather, the residuals of each student were attributed to all of the courses in which he or she had enrolled, the mean residuals for each course served as a proxy measure of student gains. Once courses were clustered by these residuals, then hypotheses were generated and tested as to why students who enrolled in a given pattern of courses experienced significant gains on one or more of the outcomes criteria (that is, the item-type residuals).

Creating a Similarity Index for Transfer and Native Groups. First, a raw data matrix was created. For the transfers, their mean residuals and the 177 courses found on five or more of their transcripts were used. The data matrix consisted of 177 columns and 9 rows. Similarly, using the mean residuals of the native group and the 300 courses found on five or more of their transcripts, a second separate raw data matrix also was created, consisting of 300 columns and 9 rows. In each data matrix, the rows represented the criterion variables: the 9 GRE item-type residual scores. The columns represented those courses enrolling five or more students. Thus, each cell value of the matrix was a mean GRE item-type score gain for those sample group students enrolling in a specific course.

Next, a similarity index (also called a resemblance matrix; see Romesburg, 1984) was created. The similarity index described how closely each course resembled the other courses according to the criterion variables: the student score residuals. So, a similarity index of 177 courses was created for the transfers and an index of 300 courses was created for the native group. The correlation coefficient (Pearson's r) was used as the measure to construct the similarity index. Thus, the correlation coefficient assessed a pattern similarity between any two courses explained in terms of the 9 GRE item-type residuals.

Results of the Cluster Analyses. Cluster analyses were performed on the similarity indices of the native and transfer groups of coursework. For each group, courses were classified into thirteen coursework patterns according to the resultant hierarchical cluster structure (see Tables 4.2 and 4.3). In fact, the choice to present the data in thirteen clusters was arbitrary. Any number of clusters can be identified depending on the hierarchical cluster structure produced; this structure remains constant regardless of the number of clusters used to form coursework patterns. A procedure for selecting the optimum number of clusters and for validating the resulting patterns is described in greater detail later in this chapter. The results of the cluster analyses and subsequent discriminant analyses for both groups suggested that student residual scores on GRE item types were strong, reliable, and robust measures in differentiating students' general learned abilities.

For the transfer group (see Table 4.2), a careful examination of courses within each cluster indicated that some courses coming from the same department appear in the same cluster. Eight of twenty-eight courses appearing in Cluster 8 came from psychology (PSY); these courses ranged from freshman- to senior-level coursework, suggesting the influence of major on the learning associated with this group. Similarly, there were apparent sequences of courses, such as the Mathematics (MAT) 211, 212, 215, and 216 sequence in Cluster 5; the association of intended sequences with gains in student learning highlights the cumulative effect of the curriculum for these students. Also, a set of courses coming from various related disciplines may form a homogeneous cluster on the basis of a set of given attributes or criteria.

For the native group (see Table 4.3), some courses from the same department appeared in the same cluster, such as the English (ENG) courses in Cluster 1, the computer information systems (CIS) in Cluster 2, and the journalism (JOURN) courses in Cluster 7. Similarly, there were apparent sequences of courses, such as the Anthropology (ANTH) 201, 202, and 203 sequence in Cluster 1. Also, a set of courses coming from various related disciplines may form a homogeneous cluster on the basis of a set of given attributes or criteria. The homogeneity of disciplines was particularly apparent in Cluster 1. Thus, while there were clear relationships between combinations and sequences of courses for both native and transfer students, it is important to note that there were different coursework patterns that were found to be associated with gains in the common learning criteria.

Discriminant Analyses of Coursework Clusters. Discriminant analyses provided secondary validation that 89.83 percent of the classification of transfer courses was correctly predicted by cluster analysis, while 81.33 percent of the classification of courses taken by native students was

Table 4.2. Coursework Patterns: Thirteen Clusters for the Transfer Group

Cluster 1 (N = 16)	Cluster 2 (N = 33)	Cluster 3 (N = 18)	Cluster 4 (N = 4)	Cluster 5 (N = 14)	Cluster 6 (N = 5)	Cluster 7 (N = 15)	Cluster 8 (N = 28)	Cluster 9 (N = 25)	Cluster 10 (N = 10)	Cluster 11 (N = 5)	Cluster 12 (N = 2)	Cluster 13 (N = 2)
AC 201	AC 201[b]	ACCT 201[b]	ANTH 100	APVC 200	ART 20[b]	ART 211[b]	BIOL 111[b]	BIO 141[b]	BIO 142[b]	EDUC 201[b]	FED 210	FI 415
ART 178[b]	AC 202[b]	ACCT 202[b]	ENGL 201[b]	APVC 300	PED 11[b]	BIO 101[b]	BIOL 112[b]	CHEM 111[b]	EC 201	ENGL 111[b]	MUS 193	PSY 314[a,b]
BA 309	AC 202	BIO 142	HIST 112[a,b]	CIS 303	PED 12[b]	FILM 370	CHEM 117	ENG 112	EC 350	ENGL 112[b]		
DM 231[a]	AC 301	CHEM 112[b]	MAT 12[b]	FED 305[a]	SOC 201[b]	GEOL 101	CIS 410[a]	ENG 201[b]	ENG 111[b]	PSYC 201[b]		
DM 310	AC 401	COMP 201[b]		FED 310[a]	SPE 401[a]	JOUR 304	CIS 480	FR 101	HIST 113[b]	PSYC 258[b]		
EC 386	AC 402	ECON 201[b]		IS 220		JOUR 308	DM 121	GEOL 102	LSM 436A			
ENG 20	BA 201	ECON 202[b]		MAT 211		JOUR 410	ENG 201	HIST 20[b]	LSM 436C			
ENG 202	BA 498	ENG 111		MAT 212		MAT 107	ENG 313	HIST 111	MAT 10[b]			
IS 201	BED 450	LSM 436		MAT 215		PHIL 301	FED 496	HIST 111[b]	MGT 450			
MGT 430	CNST 10[b]	MAT 111[b]		MAT 216		POLS 101[a]	FI 431	HIST 112	POLS 101[b]			
MGT 435	DM 122	MAT 121[b]		MUS 102		PSY 101[b]	FREN 111[b]	HIST 251[b]				
MGT 470	DM 312[a]	MUSI 211[b]		MUS 108		PSY 404	FREN 112[b]	JOUR 450[a]				
PHIL 201	DSC 122	PHED 159[b]		MUS 110		SCI 110[b]	HIST 113	MAT 102				
RE 410	DSC 310	POLI 111[b]		PHIL 211[a]		SPAN 101[b]	HIST 252	MH 310				
RE 495	DSC 312	PSY 20[b]				SPAN 111[b]	MAT 105[b]	PHED 101[b]				
SPCH 10[b]	EC 10[b]	SOCI 105[a,b]					MAT 112[a,b]	PHED 102[b]				
	EC 201[b]	SPCH 121[b]					MK 430	PSY 10[b]				
	EC 202[b]	SPCH 150					PHED 125[b]	PSY 356				
	EC 350						PHED 170[b]	PSY 358				
	ENG 112[b]						PSY 101	SOC 202[a]				
	FI 330						PSY 202	SOC 308				
	INS 350[a]						PSY 203	SPAN 202				
	IS 20[b]						PSY 204	SPCH 10[b]				
	LGLS 300						PSY 301	TH 370				
	MAT 11[b]						PSY 303	US 301				
	MGT 350						PSY 416					
	MGT 401						PSY 423					
	MK 301						SOC 201[a]					
	PED 10[b]											
	PHIL 241											
	PROG 20[b]											
	RE 301											
	SPCH 150[b]											

[a] Course misclassified according to the discriminant analysis of course clusters.

[b] Course is a transfer course from a community college.

Table 4.3. Coursework Patterns: Thirteen Clusters for the Native Group

Cluster 1 (N = 53)	Cluster 2 (N = 49)	Cluster 3 (N = 15)	Cluster 4 (N = 9)	Cluster 5 (N = 40)	Cluster 6 (N = 50)	Cluster 7 (N = 14)	Cluster 8 (N = 4)	Cluster 9 (N = 19)	Cluster 10 (N = 12)	Cluster 11 (N = 13)	Cluster 12 (N = 19)	Cluster 13 (N = 3)
AC 201	AC 202	AC 301	AC 450	AC 460[a]	APTP 200	ART 350	BIO 141[a]	BIO 325	CHEM 101	CJ 301	DM 312[a]	MAT 104[a]
AC 409	AC 451[a]	AC 401	BED 436[a]	ANTH 100	APTP 300	CJ 371	BIO 142[a]	BIO 384	DS 50[a]	CJ 311	ENG 113[a]	MGT 401[a]
ANTH 201	ANTH 102	AC 402	CIS 210[a]	APFL 200	APVC 200	HIST 113[a]	MH 310	BIO 390	DS 71[a]	CJ 321	ENG 211	SOC 308
ANTH 202	ASTR 101	AC 420	DM 122[a]	ART 101	APVC 300	HIST 476	PSY 416	CHEM 112	ENG 385	CJ 331	ENG 409	
ANTH 203	ASTR 102	APPF 100[a]	GER 201	ART 102	ART 466	JOUR 201		CHEM 117[a]	MAT 107[a]	CJ 370	ENG 435	
BL 301	BA 498	BED 456	GER 202	ART 103	BA 201	JOUR 302		CHEM 118	MAT 122	CJ 411	GEOG 350	
CJ 341	BED 450	BED 471	IS 410	ART 104	CJ 490[a]	JOUR 304		CHEM 240	MH 498	CJ 475	GER 101[a]	
CM 105	BIO 388[a]	CIS 303	MGT 450	ART 105	DM 310	JOUR 306		CHEM 241	PSY 105	CJ 494	MAT 105	
DM 231	BIO 389[a]	FED 310*	UL 301	ART 178	DSC 122[a]	JOUR 410		CHEM 242	PSY 202	DS 92	MAT 125	
DRA 370	CIS 220	JOUR 460[a]		ART 179[a]	DSC 310	JOUR 421		CHEM 460	PSY 356	ENG 201[a]	PHIL 302[a]	
DS 91	CIS 305	LGLS 405		BA 309	DSC 312	JOUR 450		ENG 315[a]	PSY 358	GEOG 101[a]	PHYS 102[a]	
EC 360	CIS 400	MAT 220		BIO 111	ENG 111[a]	JOUR 454		MAT 212[a]	PSY 404	US 301	POLS 414	
EC 386	CIS 410	MK 434		BIO 112	ENG 112[a]	JOUR 498		MAT 215		US 302	POLS 462	
ENG 202	CIS 434	MUS 320		BIO 324	FED 305	PSY 303		MAT 335			PSY 201	
ENG 208	CIS 450	RMI 350		BIO 325	GEOL 102[a]			MAT 435			PSY 314[a]	
ENG 280	CIS 460			CHEM 102	HPRD 345			MAT 451			RUS 101	
ENG 316	CIS 472			CHEM 111	IB 309			MAT 461			RUS 102	
ENG 317	CIS 480			CHEM 113	LSM 436			MAT 462			RUS 201	
ENG 370	DM 121			CHEM 116	MAT 126[a]			MGT 350[a]			SPCH 445	
EXC 401	DS 70			DS 81	MGT 430							
FED 210	DS 80			DS 90[a]	MGT 435[a]							
FR 201	DSC 104			ENG 212[a]	MGT 436							
FR 202	DSC 201			FILM 370	MGT 437[a]							
GEOL 101	EC 201			GEOG 103	MGT 439							
HIST 111	EC 202			GEOG 104	MGT 470							
HIST 112	EC 350			HRTA 310	MK 410[a]							
IS 220	ENG 313			HRTA 330	MK 420							
IS 301[a]	FI 330			HRTA 350[a]	MK 430							
IS 302	FR 101			IS 201	MK 431							
IS 400	FR 102			JOUR 101[a]	MK 451[a]							
ITAL 101	GER 102			MK 433	MUS 102							
JOUR 308	HPRD 101			MK 490	MUS 103							
JOUR 309	INS 350			MUS 105	MUS 106							
LAT 101	LGLS 300			MUS 193	MUS 108							
MAT 102	MAT 211			PHYS 101								
				PHYS 210								

MUS 393 MAT 216 POLS 320* MUS 110
PHIL 201ᵃ MAT 447 PSY 204* MUS 126
PHIL 301 MAT 448 RTP 25A   MUS 144
PHYS 230 MK 301   SPAN 10¹ MUS 145
POLS 201 PHYS 237 TH 410*   MUS 161
POLS 305ᵃ PHYS 238   MUS 191
POLS 315 PHYS 239ᵃ   MUS 244
POLS 404 POLS 101   MUS 245
SOC 202   PSY 423   MUS 246
SOC 311   RE 301   PHIL 241ᵃ
SOC 317   RTP 25   PSY 101
SOC 400ᵃ SOC 201   PSY 201
SPAN 102 SOC 316   PSY 203
SPAN 201 TH 304   PSY 301ᵃ
SPAN 202   SPCH 101
SPAN 303   SPE 401
SPCH 150ᵃ
TH 370

*Course misclassified according to the discriminant analysis of course clusters.

Note to Table 4.2 and Table 4.3: Guide to Course Rubrics

AC/ACCT	Accounting	DM	Decision Mathematics	HRTA	Hotel, Restaurant and Travel Administration	PHYS	Physics
ANTH	Anthropology	DRA	Drama	IB	International Business	POL/POLS	Political Science
APFL	Applied Music	DS	Developmental Studies	INS	Insurance	PROG	Unavailable
APPF	Applied Music	DSC	Decision Sciences	IS	Information Systems	PSY/PSYC	Psychology
APTP	Applied Music	EC	Economics	ITAL	Italian	RE	Real Estate
APVC	Applied Music	EDUC	Education	JOUR	Journalism	RTP	Regents' Test Preparation Program (Remedial)
ART	Art	ENG/ENGL	English	LAT	Latin	RUS	Russian
ASTR	Astronomy	EXC	Exceptional Children/ Special Education	LGLS	Legal Studies (Business)	SCI	Science
BA	Business Administration	FED	Foundations of Education	LSM	Library Science Media	SOC/SOCI	Sociology
BED	Business Education	FI	Finance	MAT	Mathematics	SPAN	Spanish
BIO/BIOL	Biology	FILM	Filmmaking	MGT	Management	SPCH	Speech
BL	Business Law	FR/FREN	French	MH	Mental Health	SPE	Special Education
CHEM	Chemistry	GEOG	Geography	MK	Marketing	TH	Theatre
CIS	Computer Information Systems	GEOL	Geology	MUS/MUSI	Music	UL	Urban Life
CJ	Criminal Justice	GER	German	PED	Unavailable	US	Urban Studies
CM	Commercial Music/ Recording	HIST	History	PHED	Physical Education/ Health/Recreation		
CNST	Unavailable	HPRD	Health, Physical Education, Recreation and Dance	PHIL	Philosophy		

correctly predicted. The discriminant analyses were a secondary validation, since they were based on the same sample of transcripts and test
scores. Discriminant analyses were also used to determine which courses
were correctly classified and to ascertain which item-type scores contributed to any given coursework pattern. Once the relationships between
discriminant functions and mean item-type residuals have been established, then the relationships between the discriminant functions and the
coursework clusters can also be determined. By examining the average
score of each cluster group for each discriminant function, we calculated
the extent to which each discriminant function contributes to that group.
Functions that had no correlation with specific item-type residuals were
omitted.

Each discriminant function explains a certain proportion of the variation in residual scores. Discriminant functions with strong explanatory
power, "good discriminant functions," have large between-cluster variability and low within-cluster variability (Romesburg, 1984). The eigenvalues
present the ratio of between-group to within-group sums of squares of the
residuals. Large eigenvalues are associated with the discriminant functions
that most contribute to explaining variability in GRE item-type scores.
Wilks's lambda is the ratio of the within-group sum of squares to the total
sum of the squares. It represents the proportion of the total variance in the
discriminant function values not explained by differences among cluster
groups. Wilks's lambda serves as a test of the null hypothesis that there is
no difference in the mean residuals of coursework cluster means and the
mean residual scores of the coursework in the total sample. Thus, the
eigenvalues and canonical correlations indicate the extent to which each
discriminant function contributes to our understanding of the variability
in coursework mean residuals. Lambda tests the null of the differential
coursework hypothesis for each discriminant function. Results of the
analysis indicated that a relationship did exist between coursework taken
and performance on the GRE. Certain GRE item-type residual scores
predominated.

Interpreting the Transfers' Coursework Clusters. Transfers (see
Table 4.2) who enrolled in the coursework pattern represented in Cluster
1 were more likely to improve in ability on quantitative comparisons,
analytical reasoning, and regular mathematics but were likely to decline on
logical reasoning item types. Transfer students enrolling in Cluster 2
showed high gains in quantitative comparisons and analytical reasoning.
Transfers enrolling in Cluster 3 tended to show positive gains in their
ability to answer quantitative comparisons and analytical reasoning questions. Cluster 4 had no high positive or negative association with any of the
assessment criteria. Students enrolling in Cluster 5 courses showed declines in ability on quantitative comparisons and analytical reasoning but
showed gains on logical reasoning and antonyms item types. Cluster 6

consisted of three courses. One course was misclassified. Therefore, no further analysis was conducted with this cluster. Students enrolling in Cluster 7 showed declines on quantitative comparisons and analytical reasoning item types. Cluster 8, Cluster 9, and Cluster 10 had no high positive or negative association. Students enrolling in Cluster 11 tended to decline in abilities relative to regular mathematics and antonyms. Cluster 12 consisted of two courses. One course was misclassified. Therefore, no further analysis was conducted with this cluster. Cluster 13 had no high positive or negative association with the assessment criteria.

Interpreting the Natives' Coursework Clusters. Native students (see Table 4.3) enrolling in Cluster 1 improved in antonyms and reading comprehension but declined in their analytical reasoning abilities. Natives enrolling in Cluster 2 gained in analytical reasoning but declined in antonyms. Students taking Cluster 3 coursework improved in analytical reasoning and quantitative comparisons but declined in reading comprehension. Native students enrolling in Cluster 4 showed gains in quantitative comparisons. Natives enrolled in coursework Cluster 5 gained in antonyms but declined in analytical reasoning and reading comprehension. Students signed up for Cluster 6 declined in antonyms and reading comprehension but gained in analytical reasoning. Students taking Cluster 7 gained in analytical reasoning and quantitative comparisons but declined in antonyms. Cluster 8 consisted of three courses. Two courses were misclassified. Therefore, no further analysis was conducted with this cluster. Students enrolled in Cluster 9 improved in reading comprehension, analytical reasoning, and quantitative comparisons. Students enrolling in Cluster 10 showed declines in quantitative comparisons. Students registering in Cluster 11 gained in quantitative comparisons and analytical reasoning. Students taking courses in Cluster 12 improved in reading comprehension. Cluster 13 consisted of three courses. Two courses were misclassified. Therefore, no further analysis was conducted with Clusters 12 and 13.

It should be cautioned that the association was established at the *cluster* level. No direct causal link is intimated between student enrollment in any one given course and scores on the GRE. Furthermore, at this point, one cannot say why students who enrolled in these courses had higher residuals. The cluster serves to hypothesize relationships between coursework patterns and the general learned abilities measured by the item types of the GRE. We can say that students who enrolled in specific patterns of coursework tended to evidence stronger gains on specific GRE item types, whereas others who enrolled in different coursework patterns did not tend to show such gains. This evidence affirms the hypothesis that student gains in general learned abilities are associated, positively and negatively, with the courses in which they enrolled. Further analysis is required to determine the nature of these associations.

Findings and Conclusion

Key questions are being posed about the role of the community college. University faculty and administrators do not regard highly the community college and its transfer students; many community college faculty do not hold their own students in high esteem. Defenders of the community college assert that it provides a primary avenue of opportunity in and access to higher education. Critics assert that community colleges help perpetuate the rigidity of social classes and divert bright, motivated students into dead-end occupational programs. Does the community college provide education in the first two years comparable to that of the baccalaureate-granting institution? Are credits earned at one institution equivalent to those earned at another? Can transfer student success be increased through improved articulation of courses and credits?

Adelman's (1992, p. 25) assessment of the status of research on this question is telling: "First, I am baffled by the construction of variables and estimates in most of the work bearing on this debate. Without transcripts, for example, it is nearly impossible to determine precisely who is on a transfer/academic track in a community college and who isn't. . . . Without transcripts, it is nearly impossible to determine who changed from one track to another—and when. . . . I am not sure that the construct of 'track' itself is very helpful. On so many occasions, the community college portions of student records showed individuals starting out with a combination of basic skills courses and introductions to the disciplines and professions, then selecting more and more courses in a given field, as if they were choosing a 'major.' "

This chapter used the CCAM to examine improvement in general learned abilities of transfer and native students. The goal was to determine whether the assumption underlying common course numbering schemes in statewide public higher education is valid. In short, did the courses taken at the community college produce the same effect as the comparably numbered courses at Southern University? The answer was clearly no! Different student abilities and backgrounds and different institutional environments produced different types of improvement in general learned abilities. If all undergraduates were to benefit from a single general education coursework requirement—regardless of institution of enrollment—the cluster analysis would produce such a core among all such courses taken. If common course numbering were an accurate means of identifying comparable learning experiences, then the courses taken at the community college would appear in clusters associated with the same types of gains as their counterpart courses at Southern University; this also did not occur.

Logical, discrete sets of courses were found among each group of students. The results did not support the efficacy of a statewide core curriculum or common course numbering system. Only 40 percent of the courses enrolling five or more students were part of the general education requirements and associated with gains in the transfer students' learning. Only 17 percent of the courses enrolling five or more students were part of the general education requirements and associated with improvement in the native students' learning. These findings argue against the establishment of a core curriculum as advocated by Lynne Cheney (1989). The results support the view of the advocates for distribution requirements in general education since there were differences in the gains that these students demonstrated in student incoming abilities and general learned abilities, and differences in the coursework patterns in which they enrolled. In general, community college students showed greater gains than did natives and took a more discrete set of courses from a more limited array of choices. Thus, we support the current use of a *wide range* of options in a distributional general education requirement. Instead, as our findings suggest, institutions need to identify discrete *arrays* of coursework that are more appropriate and productive for different ability levels of students. This conclusion was manifest in the findings of our analysis of transfer and native students. Discrete sets of coursework were identified that were beneficial to these students. These results suggest the need for greater academic advising in undergraduate course selection or greater prescription in the curriculum. The CCAM also can be used to identify coursework that has been beneficial to students of specific ability levels, interests, and aptitudes (Jones and Ratcliff, 1990).

In the cluster analysis of Southern University transfer and native groups, the results were comparable. Roughly eight or nine of each ten courses analyzed were accurately grouped according to differential effects in the general learned abilities of students. Enrollment in different patterns of coursework does lead to different types and levels of development as measured by the nine item types of the GRE General Test.

Student transcripts, generated from a student records data base, are powerful, nonobtrusive indicators of the curriculum experienced by undergraduates. It is recommended that the research be continued longitudinally to establish *trends* in course patterns over multiple years of graduating seniors. Through such panel studies, the extent of variation in general learning and in course-taking behavior can be established. Such research is currently under way at the National Center on Postsecondary Teaching, Learning, and Assessment at Pennsylvania State University.

Nevertheless, clear sequences and combinations of coursework do emerge from this research. Quantitative abilities are not developed solely in lower-division mathematics courses but are enhanced through an array of select applied science, social science, and business courses as well. General learning is not confined to the lower division; upper-division courses contributed strongly to the development of specific learned abilities, particularly analytical reasoning.

Native students at Southern University, as at many universities and colleges, do not have in common many formal learning experiences. From 15 to 20 percent of the coursework on one student's transcript was shared with five other students from the same sample. The lack of a common intellectual experience is only problematic to the extent that such experience is held as an institutional value. Indeed, it is the mark of a great university to preserve and advance the full landscape of fields and disciplines of inquiry. Yet, we must advance beyond the days of Charles Eliot and Ezra Cornell. The vastness of curriculum choice can be either an asset or a liability, depending on the extent to which it effectively advances student learning.

The research described here makes two significant contributions to the field of higher education. First, it provides a new way to analyze the curriculum in order to determine the most effective curriculum for students of different abilities. Second, it provides a means for examining the efficacy of articulation agreements among institutions of higher education. Both the transfer students and the native students of this study showed gains in general learned abilities. However, the nature of the courses in which they enrolled and of the gains that they evidenced was different across the two groups. The effectiveness of articulation arrangements needs further investigation, and this exploratory study provides a method and a model for such future research.

References

Adelman, C. *The Way We Are: The Community College as American Thermometer.* Washington, D.C.: Government Printing Office, 1992.

Association of American Colleges. *A New Vitality in General Education.* Washington, D.C.: Association of American Colleges, 1988.

Boyer, E. L., and Kaplan, M. *Educating for Survival.* New Rochelle, N.Y.: Change Magazine Press, 1977.

Brint, S., and Karabel, J. *The Diverted Dream: Community Colleges and the Promise of Educational Opportunity in America, 1900–1985.* New York: Oxford University Press, 1989.

Cheney, L. V. *50 Hours: A Core Curriculum for College Students.* Washington, D.C.: National Endowment for the Humanities, 1989.

Clark, B. *The School and the University.* Berkeley and Los Angeles: University of California Press, 1985.

Cohen, A. M., and Brawer, F. B. *The American Community College.* (2nd ed.) San Francisco: Jossey-Bass, 1989.

Committee on Redefining the Meaning and Purpose of Baccalaureate Degrees. Association of American Colleges. *Integrity in the College Curriculum: A Report to the Academic Community.* Washington, D.C.: Association of American Colleges, 1985.

De Ritter, L. M. "Comparative Scholastic Achievement of Native and Transfer Students." *Junior College Journal,* 1951, *21,* 83–84.

Folger, J. K., Astin, H. S., and Bayer, A. E. *Human Resources and Higher Education.* New York: Russell Sage Foundation, 1970.

Giddings, W. G. "A Study of the Performance, Progress, and Degree Achievement of Iowa Community College Transfer Students at Iowa's State Universities." Unpublished doctoral dissertation, Department of Professional Studies, Iowa State University, 1985.

Grubb, W. N. "The Decline of Community College Transfer Rates." *Journal of Higher Education*, 1991, *62*, 194–217.

Hills, J. R. "Transfer Shock: The Academic Performance of the Junior College Transfer." *Journal of Experimental Education*, 1965, *33* (3), 201–213.

Jones, E. A., and Ratcliff, J. L. "Is a Core Curriculum Best for Everybody? The Effect of Different Patterns of Coursework on the General Education of High and Low Ability College Students." Paper presented at the annual meeting of the American Educational Research Association, Boston, April 1990.

Karabel, J. "Community Colleges and Social Stratification." *Harvard Educational Review*, 1972, *42*, 521–561.

Kintzer, F. C., and Wattenbarger, J. L. *The Articulation/Transfer Phenomenon: Patterns and Directions.* Horizons Monograph Series. Washington, D.C.: American Association of Community and Junior Colleges, 1986.

Knoell, D. N., and Medsker, L. L. *From Junior to Senior College: A National Study of the Transfer Student.* Washington, D.C.: American Council on Education, 1965.

Koos, L. V. *The Junior College.* Vol. 1. Minneapolis: University of Minnesota Press, 1924.

Levine, A. *Handbook on Undergraduate Curriculum: Prepared for the Carnegie Council on Policy Studies in Higher Education.* San Francisco: Jossey-Bass, 1978.

National Endowment for the Humanities. *To Reclaim a Legacy: A Report on the Humanities in Higher Education.* Washington, D.C.: National Endowment for the Humanities, 1984.

Nickens, J. M. "Transfer Shock or Transfer Ecstasy?" Paper presented at the annual meeting of the American Educational Research Association, Chicago, April 1972. (ED 061 925)

Pascarella, E. T. "College Environmental Influences on Learning and Cognitive Development: A Critical Review and Synthesis." In J. Smart (ed.), *Higher Education: Handbook of Theory and Research.* Vol. 1. New York: Agathon, 1985.

Ratcliff, J. L. "Determining the Effects of Different Coursework Patterns on the General Student Learning at Four Colleges and Universities." Paper presented at the annual meeting of the American Educational Research Association, San Francisco, March 1989.

Richardson, R. C., and Doucette, D. S. *Persistence, Performance, and Degree Achievement of Arizona's Community College Transfers in Arizona's Public Universities.* Tempe: Department of Higher and Adult Education, Arizona State University, 1980. (ED 197 785)

Romesburg, H. C. *Cluster Analysis for Researchers.* Belmont, Calif.: Lifelong Learning, 1984.

Snyder, T. D. *Digest of Education Statistics, 1989.* Washington, D.C.: National Center for Educational Statistics, 1989.

Study Group on the Conditions of Excellence in American Higher Education. National Institute of Education. *Involvement in Learning: Realizing the Potential of American Higher Education.* Washington, D.C.: Government Printing Office, 1984.

Terenzini, P. T. "Assessment with Open Eyes: Pitfalls in Studying Student Outcomes." *Journal of Higher Education*, 1989, *60* (6), 644–703.

JAMES L. RATCLIFF *is professor of higher education and director of the Center for the Study of Higher Education at Pennsylvania State University, University Park. He also is executive director of the National Center on Postsecondary Teaching, Learning, and Assessment, and editor of the* Journal of General Education.

In the study described here, faculty members from three institutions disclosed select dimensions of their courses.

Faculty Goals and Methods of Instruction: Approaches to Classroom Assessment

David S. Guthrie

In less formal moments, curious students may ask their professors, "So what is it that you really do?" At a time when state and federal governments, accreditation agencies, private associations, and the public at large are demanding increased accountability from the academic enterprise, answers to this question take on considerable significance. Further, understanding how and why college faculty do what they do is equally important. Building on the differential coursework patterns project discussed by Ratcliff (this volume, Chapters One and Four) and Jones (this volume, Chapter Three), I address these questions in this chapter by examining faculty members' perceptions regarding the instructional process and the syllabi and tests that they employ to organize and evaluate their respective courses.

My colleagues and I collected these data from a sample of faculty members from a research university (Stanford University), a comprehensive college (Ithaca College), and a liberal arts women's college (Mills College). These faculty, most of whom were full-time (94 percent of the sample), represent an even distribution of academic rank (full, associate, and assistant professors). However, one particularly distinctive characteristic of these faculty and their courses must be noted. We intentionally selected faculty who taught classes that, when compared to other professors and courses, produced students who demonstrated the highest gains in cognitive abilities, particularly analytical reasoning. Prior to the study, we anticipated that these gains were due to the higher-level goals, objec-

NEW DIRECTIONS FOR HIGHER EDUCATION, no. 80, Winter 1992   © Jossey-Bass Publishers

tives, learning tasks, and testing designs employed by these faculty members. In short, we wanted to know what it was about these faculty members' goals and methods of instruction that accounted for exemplary student performance.

The results that follow are organized into three main topical sections corresponding to Tyler's (1950) long-established design for college curriculum. The focus of the first section is the goals of faculty instruction. The second section concerns the modes of instruction used by faculty members. And the final section examines the nature of student evaluation.

Goals of Faculty Instruction

A large majority of faculty members sampled (90 percent) explained that they were solely responsible for setting the goals and content of their courses. As Bergquist, Gould, and Greenberg (1981, p. 144) explain, this finding is consistent with the course-planning practices of most colleges and universities: "Faculty-planned curriculums are pervasive and respond to the legitimate need of students for clear and detailed information about the courses they will take and the courses of study they will follow for particular careers." Realizing this, however, how do faculty members describe their specific goals for the courses that they teach? What is it that they expect to accomplish in the classroom?

According to our composite findings, the primary objective of classroom instruction is to "have students learn course content." (Later, I discuss how this central purpose was manifested in the strong emphasis that the faculty members placed on students' cognitive development in their final evaluations.) It also should be noted, however, that differences existed among the faculty at the three institutions. For example, a very small percentage of the Mills faculty in the sample (12 percent), particularly when compared to the Stanford (43 percent) and Ithaca (41 percent) faculty members, considered "[having] students learn course content" their primary education objective. A considerable percentage of the Mills faculty members (44 percent), owing at least in part to Mills's stated mission as a single-gender institution, considered "[having] students learn a particular perspective on course content" their primary instructional purpose. In contrast, 31 percent of Stanford faculty and only 12 percent of Ithaca faculty shared this goal.

The purpose of teaching considered least important by the largest percentage of faculty members (35 percent) was "assisting students to incorporate certain skills and/or knowledge into their daily, personal lives." On closer inspection at the institutional level, however, considerable differences surfaced again. That is, only 20 percent of Mills faculty members and only 25 percent of Ithaca faculty viewed this objective as least important, while 52 percent of Stanford faculty eschew the significance of this objective. As I later discuss, this finding reflects the tendency of a majority of Stanford faculty members, and substantially lesser percentages of faculty members at Mills and Ithaca, to be more concerned with students' development of lower-order cognitive skills such as knowledge acquisition and comprehension than with higher-order skills such as integration, application, and evaluation.

Notwithstanding the prevalent differences among the faculty at these three institutions regarding the goals of instruction, faculty members at each institution were articulate about their expectations for their courses. As a result, students' gains in cognitive abilities, including analytical reasoning, may be attributable to the clear understanding that they received from their professors regarding the expected goals of the respective courses. A more complete picture of this dynamic process was provided by our examination of the modes of instruction utilized by the sample faculty at these institutions.

Modes of Instruction

Modes of instruction not only refers to a professor's pedagogical style but includes who actually performs the teaching and the instructional materials used as well. Each of these dimensions of classroom instruction has a profound impact on what students learn.

Pedagogical Style. Faculty members responded to two questions that were designed with reference to Axelrod's (1973) model of didactic and evocative modes of teaching or pedagogical styles. A didactic mode of teaching has as its goal a mastery of a definite body of knowledge. The emphasis in this model is on the acquisition of knowledge or skills primarily through memorization; a teacher's goal is "to develop in the student an automatic or semiautomatic response" (Axelrod, 1973, p. 11). In contrast, the evocative mode of teaching is concerned with inquiry and discovery strategies. From this perspective, the teacher may be thought of as an artist who creates an atmosphere for learning by promoting student's encounters with each component of the teaching-learning process: teacher, learner, and subject matter.

Most of the faculty in our sample (57 percent) believed that an evocative mode best represented their teaching approach. The second single largest percentage of faculty (24 percent) sought a balance in their teaching between the evocative and didactic modes. Many of the faculty in the sample objected to a distinction between these two "poles," calling the distinction arbitrary and stating that learning involves both content acquisition and development of thinking processes. Consequently, a large majority of the faculty contended that they employed pedagogical styles— either evocative or some combination of evocative and didactic—that were designed to challenge students to develop far more than lower-order cognitive abilities. As such, faculty members' self-reported pedagogical styles may have contributed, in an inordinate way, to the gains attributed to the students in their classes.

Who Teaches? We asked respondents to state who typically is involved in teaching their courses (see Table 5.1). In most cases, instruction was performed by the individual faculty members (88 percent). However, we also found that teaching assistants (TAs) and team teaching were utilized in some courses (20 percent and 11 percent, respectively), particularly at Stanford (41 percent and 24 percent, respectively) and most often in the biological and physical sciences. The presence of a significant number of TAs at Stanford is characteristic of larger, research universities. At Stanford, the TAs read student papers and projects, graded student examinations according to criteria established by faculty, and provided primary feedback to students on their performance in the courses. The fact that team teaching occurs more frequently at research universities such as Stanford and that, as discussed in the next section, a majority of the Stanford faculty sampled were concerned with the development of students' lower-order cognitive skills is noteworthy. One wonders whether some aspect or style of team teaching actually may be detrimental to the development of college students' higher-order cognitive skills.

One additional observation can be made about who teaches college courses. Our findings support Bergquist, Gould, and Greenberg's (1981) contention that professional staff members are often "overlooked" instructional resources. As our respondents reported, professional staff personnel (including administrators) were rarely called on to develop and teach courses (3 percent overall) despite their rich experiences, expertise, and insight on particular subjects. Student peer teaching (7 percent) and student self-instruction (6 percent) were uncommon practices as well, particularly at Stanford as compared to Mills and Ithaca.

Instructional Materials. This study supports the notion that books, journals, newspapers, and the like constitute "the primary instructional

Table 5.1. Actual Course Teachers

Instructor(s)	Stanford (N = 92)	Ithaca (N = 106)	Mills (N = 41)	Total (N = 239)
Faculty member	74	97	95	88
Team teaching	24	4	0	11
Shared teaching, alternate days	1	1	0	1
Teaching assistant	41	7	5	20
Professional staff	0	4	7	3
Student peer assistant	2	8	15	7
Student self-instruction	2	9	7	6

Note: Table figures are percentages of interview respondents.

materials" (Bergquist, Gould, and Greenberg, 1981, p. 96) used by most faculty members (91 percent) (see Table 5.2). Various forms of video technology were also used by faculty members (54 percent). For example, the syllabi analysis revealed that audiovisual cassettes were common instructional methods. Although an instructor's lack of knowledge or skill at one time may have prevented him or her from using this equipment, more faculty are now effectively using this media in their classrooms. In the same way, computer technology seems to be growing in popularity, even though only a relatively small number of our respondents (20 percent) included it.

In addition, significant numbers of faculty interviewees explained that they used laboratories and studios (21 percent), simulated environments (17 percent), and experiential learning (20 percent) as instructional devices. The examination of a sample of course syllabi, for example, indicated that one of the interviewees required students to spend several days at a physical therapy clinic; other faculty members required the completion of weekly laboratory homework assignments. Many of the instructors who included these instructional methods were in the physical, biological, or behavioral sciences, engineering, and the performing arts. Based on gains in the cognitive abilities of the students in the courses that we examined, as well as the responses obtained in the faculty interviews, the inclusion of additional instructional materials beyond the conventional use of print medium seems to enhance the overall educational development of college students.

Evaluation of Student Learning

One of the primary responsibilities of faculty members across the country is evaluation of what students are learning in their classes. In this section, I examine two particular components of the evaluation process: how learning is assessed and the nature of student evaluation.

Table 5.2. Instructional Methods Used by Faculty Members

Method	Stanford (N = 92)	Ithaca (N = 106)	Mills (N = 41)	Total (N = 239)
Print medium	89	92	93	91
Audio technology	12	26	17	19
Video technology	46	61	54	54
Computer technology	25	21	10	20
Laboratories/Studios	18	23	24	21
Simulated environments	11	25	12	17
Experiential learning	16	26	12	20
Field trips	6	4	15	7

Note: Table figures are percentages of interview respondents.

How Learning Is Assessed. Most faculty members in our sample used multiple measures of evaluation to assess student learning (see Table 5.3). The sample syllabi analysis confirmed our survey data indicating that various combinations of tests, papers, class participation and attendance, and projects typically served as the criteria for student evaluation. Tests were the most common assessment tool (89 percent). It should be noted, however, that the Mills faculty were less likely than their counterparts at Ithaca and Stanford to use tests as an assessment tool, and more likely to use papers and presentations/performances. From the sample test analysis, we found that course tests most often were objective in nature, in that they consisted of multiple-choice, true-false, matching, and short answer questions. Essay questions and problems or computations also were present in the sample of tests, but not as frequently and with less comparative weight. Other common evaluation tools used by faculty members in the study were papers (43 percent) and projects (26 percent).

Nature of Student Evaluation. How the faculty members evaluated student learning (Table 5.3) took on considerable importance as soon as we examined how they constructed the contours of evaluation. The work of several curriculum and learning theorists guided the development of our interview questions concerning the evaluation of student learning. Specifically, we used Bloom's (1956) cognitive domain taxonomy, Krathwohl, Bloom, and Masia's (1964) affective domain taxonomy, and Simpson's (1972) psychomotor domain taxonomy to construct appropriate queries about how faculty members assess students' performance. As the term is used here, a *taxonomy* denotes a classification of various goals of the education process that is intended to assist educators with the design and evaluation of course curricula. A *domain* simply refers to a specific category or arena of educational development.

Table 5.3. How Learning Was Assessed by Faculty Members

Medium	Stanford (N = 92)	Ithaca (N = 106)	Mills (N = 41)	Total (N = 239)
Tests	91	92	73	89
Papers	36	45	56	43
Projects	16	36	22	26
Presentations/Performances	9	35	46	27
Homework	16	3	7	9
Laboratory assignments	5	6	0	5
Participation/Attendance	1	10	10	7
Other	1	7	7	5

Note: Table figures are percentages of interview respondents.

A brief description of each of the domains mentioned above is instructive. The cognitive domain describes education outcomes that require "the recall or recognition of knowledge and the development of intellectual abilities and skills" (Bloom, 1956, p. 7). An example of an education outcome within the cognitive domain is a student's ability to remember dates, events, persons, or similar bits of information.

The affective domain consists of education objectives that are linked with a student's "interests, attitudes, appreciations, values, and emotional sets or biases" (Krathwohl, 1964, p. 7). An individual's active participation in class discussions is a classic example of an education outcome within the affective domain.

Finally, the psychomotor domain is composed of education goals that focus on "some muscular or motor skill, some manipulation of material and objects, or some act which requires a neuromuscular co-ordination" (Krathwohl, 1964, p. 7). For instance, an education outcome that characterizes the psychomotor domain is a student's ability to conduct a physical procedure with consistency, such as conducting a laboratory experiment, performing an interpretive dance, or playing a musical instrument.

During the interviews, faculty members indicated the degrees to which the final evaluations of their students were based on each of the three primary areas discussed above: cognitive, affective, and psychomotor performances. The majority of faculty respondents (68 percent) across the three institutions in the study based 80 percent or more of their final evaluations on students' cognitive development. Among the institutions, Stanford had the largest percentage of faculty (76 percent) in this response category, followed by Ithaca (65 percent) and Mills (56 percent). Although marked differences existed among the three institutions (owing, at least in part, to differences in institutional missions), a majority of those interviewed at each institution believed that students' cognitive development is vital to the education process. Simply stated, most of the faculty members viewed students' cognitive development as *the* legitimate basis for test construction and course evaluation.

The proportion of faculty members who based their final evaluations on students' affective development was small. In fact, the largest percentage of surveyed faculty (45 percent), representing a wide array of courses, remarked that students' affective development constituted less than 10 percent of their final evaluations. Moreover, only 14 percent of faculty respondents stated that they included students' affective performance as more than 30 percent of the final grades. Most of these faculty taught in either traditional liberal arts disciplines (for example, English, economics, history, chemistry, sociology, and literature) or applied fields (for example, business, government, and engineering). Approximately 28 percent of the faculty used students' affective performance as 10 to 20 percent of the final grades. This corresponds with a finding from the syllabi analysis, in which 26 percent of a sample of course syllabi included class participation and attendance as 10 to 20 percent of the final evaluations of students. On the whole, then, these findings underscore faculty members' infrequent utilization of noncognitive measures to evaluate students' development.

Even more diminutive was the percentage of faculty members' final evaluations that were based on psychomotor competencies. A large majority of the faculty (82 percent) observed that students' psychomotor development was *not* a criterion for final evaluation. This finding is understandable given that the development of psychomotor abilities was not an expected outcome in the courses that composed a large portion of the sample. Only 18 percent of the faculty members included psychomotor performance as a basis for final evaluation, and most of these individuals based 20 percent or less of the final grades on students' psychomotor development. Faculty members who placed greater emphasis (50 percent or higher) on psychomotor competencies in determining students' final grades were members of performance disciplines such as music, drama, or dance. The clear appropriateness of employing evaluation strategies that measure students' psychomotor performances in these particular courses may explain, at least in part, the observed student gains.

The survey also elicited faculty members' responses to more specific dimensions of their evaluations of students' cognitive, affective, and psychomotor development by asking them to rate the importance that they attached in their overall evaluations to select student abilities (using a Likert-type scale). A majority of interviewed faculty members across the three institutions considered the evaluation of students to be very important in two particular cognitive development areas: (1) gaining basic knowledge, language, or terms and (2) understanding concepts, theories, and trends of the field of study. The areas of cognitive competence ranked least important in faculty members' evaluations of students were, in decreasing order of importance, students' ability to judge the worth or value of something based on specific criteria, students' ability to distinguish between facts and inferences, and students' ability to perform, act out, and demonstrate skills involved in the field of study.

These findings, which the analysis of a sample of class tests and syllabi corroborated, suggest that students' final evaluations were based most often on the development of lower-order cognitive abilities (for example, knowledge acquisition and comprehension) rather than on the development of higher-order cognitive abilities (for example, application, analysis, synthesis, and evaluation) (Bloom, 1976). Based on our expectation, stated at the outset of the chapter, that these courses may have produced greater student gains in cognitive ability because the faculty who taught them expected higher-order proficiencies, these findings are quite puzzling. Further, at a time when higher education is being called on to deliver an educational experience that makes integrative connections, links learning with civic responsibility, and engages students to be benevolent problem solvers within an increasingly complex and multicultural world, these results are also sobering. Perhaps the instructional approach of the faculty who taught these courses challenged students to develop higher-order cognitive abilities even though the evaluation measures created by these faculty members fell short in this regard.

As noted earlier, most of the faculty members interviewed did not base a large portion of their final evaluations on students' affective development. This finding is reflected as well in faculty members' responses regarding their evaluations of specific affective abilities in students. Almost one-half of the faculty members across the three institutions considered only two particular components of students' affective development to be important (both components relate to class participation). These faculty members were not confined to a small number of specific subject areas but instead represented a wide array of disciplines and fields. On the whole, Mills College faculty placed greater emphasis on evaluating students' affective development than did the faculty at either Stanford or Ithaca. Once again, this finding ostensibly indicates differences regarding institutional mission and values, particularly with regard to institutional expectations for classroom dynamics.

As might be expected given earlier comments, students' psychomotor development played even less of a role in the final evaluations according to faculty members. As a result, a majority of interviewees (ranging between 71 percent and 73 percent) explained that none of the seven specific psychomotor development areas included in the survey was important in their final evaluations of students. Only those faculty members who taught in fields such as physical education, music education, drama, dance, engineering, and chemistry—subjects that typically require some type of physical proficiency—considered the development of psychomotor skills important to students' learning processes.

Based on the discussion above, several summary comments are pertinent. First, faculty members clearly placed a primary emphasis on students' cognitive development in their evaluation practices. Second, while class participation was generally valued, its relative weight in determining students' final grades was slight. Third, students' psychomotor development was assessed only in courses that traditionally require such competence. Finally, but perhaps most important, faculty members' evaluation practices, on the whole, did not reflect an interest in testing higher-level reasoning abilities. Although students may have emerged from these courses with comparatively higher gains in cognitive skills, they generally were not asked to demonstrate their increased proficiencies in the tests that they took.

Conclusion

The findings on faculty members' evaluations of students' cognitive development and the findings on the nature of faculty members' purposes in teaching, when compared, present a confused picture. On the one hand, faculty members at all three institutions rated students' ability to "gain basic knowledge, language, or terms" and to "understand concepts, theories, and trends of the field of study" as very important components of their final evaluations. These findings are most characteristic of a didactic teaching-learning process. On the other hand, a majority of surveyed faculty members (57 percent) stated that their teaching approach may be identified as "teaching 'thinking processes.' " This finding corresponds with their stated preference for an evocative teaching-learning mode. Thus, it appears that many of the faculty members saw themselves as evocative "artists," although their course objectives and evaluation procedures were clearly didactic.

Similarly, a considerable gap also was apparent between faculty members' education goals and their modes of instruction. According to Bergquist, Gould, and Greenberg (1981), content-base teaching, or what Axelrod (1973) refers to as the didactic mode, includes the following instructional methods: lecturing, reading, question-and-answer exercises, and audiovisual instruction. In contrast, interaction-based teaching (Bergquist, Gould, and Greenberg, 1981), or what Axelrod (1973) terms the evocative mode, includes the following instructional methods: team teaching, laboratory/studio, simulations, seminar/discussion, case study, role playing, and in-class discussions. It is immediately apparent which instructional methods—those most common to content-based teaching or those most common to interaction-based teaching—were most prevalent among the faculty members surveyed in this study.

Clearly, a certain incongruence exists in many of the faculty members' self-perceptions. Notwithstanding apparent institutional variations, many of those interviewed saw themselves as interaction-based or evocative teachers whose expressed primary purpose in the learning process was to teach students thinking processes. In reality, however, these faculty members fulfilled their roles as content-based or didactic teachers whose day-to-day actions were geared to transmit knowledge to students. The point here is not to evaluate the comparative "goodness" or "badness" of the evocative or didactic modes of teaching. Rather, the important issue is to affirm that teaching involves much more than simply talking about what one knows or managing the classroom effectively. As Shulman (1987) explained, exemplary teachers continually weave together threads of what they know, how they know, and how they articulate what and how they know to students. From this perspective, dynamic teaching "begins with an act of reason, continues with a process of reasoning, culminates in performances of imparting, eliciting, involving, or enticing, and is then thought about some more until the process can begin again" (Shulman, 1987, p. 13).

Based on the findings of the present study, some faculty members' instructional goals, modes of teaching, and evaluation practices apparently do not intersect in the classroom. Although subsequent analysis has indicated that this pedagogical schizophrenia is partly explained by differences in institutional mission, many faculty members nevertheless may be unable "to transform the content knowledge he or she possesses into forms that are pedagogically powerful" (Shulman, 1987, p. 15). At an individual or group level, therefore, faculty members must become more fully conscious and conscientious regarding the linkages between self-perceived education purposes and actual course objectives, instructional methods, pedagogy, and student evaluation. In short, what Lindquist (1978) refers to as the "performance gap" must be closed. Clearly, many faculty members effectively and creatively teach college students sophisticated thinking processes, as demonstrated by the gains in cognitive abilities among the students in this study. Other faculty members, however, believe that they are teaching thinking processes but actually may be insipidly transmitting knowledge and testing students' short-term memory skills. The educational experiences of today's college students will be improved to the extent that faculty members come to terms not only with the expert grasp of their discipline or field but also with how they fashion and communicate what they know in college classrooms, including their goals and approaches for evaluating student performance.

At the institutional level, colleges and universities must investigate new approaches to education delivery. How much longer can institutions afford to offer classes at traditional times and frequencies and in traditional places and still meet the seemingly inexorable diversification of student needs and interests? If Birnbaum (1983, p. 179) is correct that "the maintenance and enhancement of diversity are critical to the future stability and responsiveness of the American system of higher education," then institutions must reconcile the appropriateness of the structures, contexts, and methods of their academic systems. Institutions also must build greater consensus among institutional participants regarding the relationships among these components of academic life. Moreover, "involving" (Kuh, Schuh, Whitt, and Associates, 1991) institutions that seek to "reclaim [and, might I add, maintain] the public trust" (as the theme of the 1992 American Association for Higher Education Conference touted) must continually, and with great wisdom, examine the full scope of their educational enterprise to ensure that their graduates fully benefit from the college experience.

References

Axelrod, J. *The University Teacher as Artist*. San Francisco: Jossey-Bass, 1973.

Bergquist, W. H., Gould, R. A., and Greenberg, E. M. *Designing Undergraduate Education: A Systematic Guide*. San Francisco: Jossey-Bass, 1981.

Birnbaum, R. *Maintaining Diversity in Higher Education*. San Francisco: Jossey-Bass, 1983.

Bloom, B. S. (ed.). *Taxonomy of Educational Objectives*. Handbook I: *Cognitive Domain*. New York: McKay, 1956.

Bloom, B. S. *Human Characteristics and Learning*. New York: McGraw-Hill, 1976.

Krathwohl, D. R., Bloom, B. S., and Masia, B. *Taxonomy of Educational Objectives*. Handbook II: *Affective Domain*. New York: McKay, 1964.

Kuh, G. D., Schuh, J. H., Whitt, E. J., and Associates. *Involving College: Successful Approaches to Fostering Student Learning and Development Outside the Classroom*. San Francisco: Jossey-Bass, 1991.

Lindquist, J. *Strategies for Change*. Berkeley, Calif.: Pacific Soundings Press, 1978.

Shulman, L. S. "Knowledge and Teaching: Foundations of the New Reform." *Harvard Educational Review*, 1987, 57 (1), 1–22.

Simpson, E. J. *The Classification of Educational Objectives in the Psychomotor Domain*. Vol. 3. Washington, D.C.: Gryphon House, 1972.

Tyler, R. W. *Basic Principles of Curriculum and Instruction*. Chicago: University of Chicago Press, 1950.

DAVID S. GUTHRIE is dean of student development at Calvin College, Grand Rapids, Michigan.

In the study described here, faculty discussed how they strive to improve student learning, and their course materials provide useful illustrations.

How Faculty Promote Cognitive Development in Their Students

Elizabeth A. Jones

The value of assessments of student learning is the guidance that they provide toward more effective educational programs and, ultimately, toward improved student performance in college. For assessments to be of value in improving student learning, they must not simply tell us how well students have learned but also link that learning to students' educational experiences. While the evidence suggests that most colleges and universities are trying to improve student learning, the results of their efforts have yet to materialize (Astin, 1991; Eaton, 1991).

The curriculum at many institutions such as comprehensive colleges and research universities is necessarily complex and often consists of hundreds or thousands of course choices for students. These course choices represent the variation in the incoming ability of the students, the expanding knowledge base in the disciplines and fields of study, and the dynamics of faculty experimentation and reform of the curriculum. All of these forces make the identification and selection of appropriate coursework for students difficult. However, faculty and students need information about what particular sets of courses strengthen student learning. Once we identify courses associated with improvements in student learning, then we can talk with individual faculty to explore the ways in which their course plans and assessments of student learning contribute to these improvements. This chapter provides an overview of the different ways in which faculty strive to improve student learning.

The Coursework Cluster Analysis Model (CCAM) is a technique that identifies particular groups of courses that enhance student learning. The methods are fully described by Ratcliff (this volume, Chapter One). In short, Ratcliff and I used a CCAM statistical procedure to link courses that students took to the gains in learning that they evidenced through outcomes assessment. Once we identified these coursework patterns, we interviewed the faculty who actually taught these particular courses. We wanted to determine the ways in which these faculty organized their courses, what they expected of their students, and how they assessed student learning. We collected course syllabi and examinations from these faculty as we interviewed them. We asked them if they believed that their own courses helped students to improve certain cognitive abilities (namely, analytical reasoning, reading comprehension, and mathematics) and how their courses helped. In addition, we explored the advice that these faculty gave to students who wanted to improve their abilities. The results of our faculty interviews provide insights into the interrelationships among individual courses and their associations with improvement in students' general learned abilities. We discovered that these faculty planned their courses and assessed student learning in ways that contributed to improvements in student learning.

Assessments of Student Abilities

One means of assessing gains in student learning is the Graduate Record Examination (GRE) completed by graduating seniors. The GRE General Test is designed to describe the student's broad verbal, mathematics, and analytical abilities. However, nine individual item types serve as discrete measures of students' general learned abilities. They include analogies, sentence completion, reading comprehension, antonyms, quantitative comparisons, regular mathematics, data interpretation, logical reasoning, and analytical reasoning. The GRE assesses student cognitive abilities that cut across a variety of disciplines rather than content learning of a particular field.

In our study, we measured the gains that students experienced in these nine areas from the time they entered college to the time of the GRE testing during their senior year. These measures assessed important skills. For example, analytical reasoning is closely tied to the national goal of improving college graduates' abilities to think critically. The improvement of these skills is critical if we are to help our college graduates become effective citizens and employees. These skills are also important to the success of our graduates as they compete in an increasingly global society.

Reading comprehension and analytical reasoning were the two types of general learned ability areas where improvements in student learning occurred. For the reading comprehension area, students were asked to read narratives with "understanding, insight, and discrimination." These passages challenged a student's ability to analyze using a variety of perspectives, "including the ability to recognize both explicitly stated elements in the passage and assumptions underlying statements or arguments in the passage as well as the implications of those statements or arguments" (Educational Testing Service, 1987, p. 31). The assessment of these types of abilities are critical to the achievement of the nation's education goals. In order for students to improve their writing and critical thinking skills, they must be able to comprehend and understand written material.

The analytical reasoning items of the GRE are designed to measure a student's ability "to understand a given structure of arbitrary relationships among fictitious persons, places, things, or events, and to deduce new information from the relationships" (Educational Testing Service, 1987, p. 38). Through our interviews with faculty who taught the courses associated with improvements in student learning, we discovered that these faculty formally encouraged the development of reading comprehension and analytical reasoning through the assignments and examinations that they required their students to complete.

We presented these faculty with examples of different types of questions representative of each of the nine types of questions in the GRE General Test. They were asked to identify which types of questions their own courses would help students to answer by strengthening their general learned abilities. In most cases, faculty selected the same types of questions with which their courses had been identified using the CCAM. Faculty viewed their own individual courses as making contributions to improvements in certain areas of student learning. In this chapter, reading comprehension and analytical reasoning are the two areas where faculty examples and illustrations indicate how they have strived to improve these abilities. Most faculty are usually motivated and eager to improve student learning. Therefore, they are attracted to assessment results in general and to a method for linking those results to specific outcomes. The faculty interviewed in our study wanted to learn how their own individual courses contributed to gains in student learning.

Reading Comprehension

Most of the faculty interviewed were pleased that someone took an interest in their classes and teaching. They were happy to articulate how they strived to develop these learned abilities in their own courses. One English professor in our sample taught her students to read texts carefully in an introductory English literature course. Students learned to identify the main ideas and supporting statements by searching for clues in the texts. They also learned to differentiate statements and to discover their different implications. An economics professor who taught a microeconomics class used sets of minicases to apply the material learned through assigned readings. An advertising professor required students to read the *New York Times* on a regular basis. A mathematics professor primarily used word problems in his basic mathematics course assignments. Overall, these faculty were able to discern relationships between their own individual courses and student improvements in analytical reasoning ability.

Our review of sample faculty examinations revealed items that were closely related to reading comprehension. Exhibit 6.1 is an actual reading comprehension item in the GRE. This item is similar to examples taken from two course examinations in our sample. A professor's examination in the course Fundamentals of Psychology and another professor's examination in the course Introduction to Business both contained items that assessed reading comprehension abilities (see Exhibit 6.2). These two faculty members, like the others in our sample, viewed their own courses as aiding students in reading comprehension. The test items in Exhibit 6.2 evidence that the faculty did evaluate their students' ability to comprehend narrative and the implications of the material.

Exhibit 6.1. Reading Comprehension Item from the Graduate Record Examination

Reading Comprehension
(Reading to understand a written passage from several perspectives.)

Directions: Each passage in this group is followed by questions based on its content. After reading a passage, choose the best answer to each question. Answer all questions following a passage on the basis of what is stated or implied in that passage.

Initially the Vinaver theory that Malory's eight romances, once thought to be fundamentally unified, were in fact eight independent works produced both a sense of relief and an unpleasant shock. Vinaver's theory comfortably explained away the apparent contradictions of chronology and made each romance independently satisfying. It was, however, disagreeable to find that what had been thought of as one book was now eight books. Part of this response was the natural reaction to the disturbance of set ideas. Nevertheless, even now, after lengthy consideration of the theory's refined but legitimate observations, one cannot avoid the conclusion that the eight romances are only one work. It is not quite a matter of disagreeing with the theory of independence, but of rejecting its implications: that the romances may be taken in any or not one particular order, that they have no cumulative effect, and that they are as separate as the works of a modern novelist.

The primary purpose of the passage is to
  a. Discuss the validity of a hypothesis. [correct answer]
  b. Summarize a system of general principles.
  c. Propose guidelines for future argument.
  d. Stipulate conditions for acceptance of an interpretation.
  e. Deny accusations about an apparent contradiction.

Source: GRE test items selected from GRE General Test, Edition GR87-5, Educational Testing Service, (1987). Reprinted by permission of Educational Testing Service.

Disclaimer: Permission to reprint GRE materials does not constitute review or endorsement by Educational Testing Service of this publication as a whole or of any other testing information it may contain.

Exhibit 6.2. Items Assessing
Reading Comprehension from Course Examinations

Psychology

Mary takes a course in which she is tested every two weeks. Her studying falls off right after a test, followed by a gradual increase to a rapid rate of studying as the next test approaches. Her studying conforms to the typical pattern of responding maintained on (blank) schedules.

   a. fixed-ratio
   b. variable-ratio
   c. fixed-interval
   d. variable-interval

Business

Twenty nonunion employees of the American Telephone and Telegraph Company (AT&T) and the Chesapeake and Potomac Telephone Company (C&P) filed suit against the Communication Workers of America (CWA) in 1986. AT&T and C&P maintained labor agreements of containing agency shop provisions with the union. In their lawsuit the nonunion employees in the bargaining unit objected to CWA's use of their agency fees for the purposes unrelated to collective bargaining, contract administration, or grievance adjustments. The judge found CWA guilty of misusing agency shop dues. In her findings the judge should have indicated that CWA action violated the

   a. Taft-Hartley Act
   b. Norris-LaGuardia Act
   c. Wagner Act
   d. Ladrum-Griffin Act
   e. Fair Labor Standards Act

Analytical Reasoning

Some faculty in our sample believed that their courses helped students to improve in analytical reasoning. One professor stated that through a major written paper in his introductory political science course, students analyzed a situation such as the Vietnam War and had to make a written case of whether it was winnable. A business professor stated that her consumer behavior course helped students since they had to interpret changing environmental conditions and draw conclusions about how these conditions impacted on certain marketing problems. A science professor thought that his introductory biology course helped students improve their analytical reasoning abilities through the extensive number of clinical decisions that the students were required to make.

Our review of sample faculty examinations revealed items that were closely tied to analytical reasoning. Exhibit 6.3 is an actual analytical reasoning item in the GRE. This item is similar to examples taken from two course examinations in our sample. A professor's examination in the course Introduction to Philosophy and another professor's examination in the course Engineering Economics both assessed analytical reasoning (see Exhibit 6.4). These two examples indicate links between coursework and the faculty members' evaluations of students' ability to understand a structure of relationships to deduce information (Educational Testing Service, 1988). We did not interview faculty about all of the courses that they taught, just those courses that the CCAM showed to be related to gains in analytical reasoning or reading comprehension. Similarly, we did not interview all of the faculty, only those who taught courses associated with gains in analytical reasoning or reading comprehension.

The information gained from these faculty who taught courses associated with improvements in student learning can be instructive for other peers. They can serve as mentors and can provide informative examples from their course syllabi, class assignments, and assessment methods. These materials can be shared with colleagues who seek to foster similar types of abilities in their own students. Teams of faculty seeking common goals such as the improvement of students' ability to think critically could serve as a network of collaborators who explore ways to improve the curriculum based on the assessment results.

Exhibit 6.3. Analytical Reasoning Item from the Graduate Record Examination

Analytical Reasoning
(Understanding a given structure of relationships, deduction of new information, and assessment of the conditions used to establish the structure.)

Directions: Each question or group of questions is based on a passage or set of conditions. In answering some of the questions, it may be useful to draw a rough diagram. For each question, select the best answer choice given.

Exactly twelve books are arranged from left to right on a shelf. Of the twelve books, four are small paperback books, two are large paperback books, three are clothbound books, and three are leatherbound books. The four small paperback books are next to each other, and the three leatherbound books are next to each other. The first (leftmost) book and the twelfth (rightmost) book are paperback books.

If the third book is a small paperback book and each large paperback book is next to a leatherbound book, which of the following books must be a large paperback book?
   a. The first
   b. The second
   c. The sixth
   d. The eighth [correct answer]
   e. The eleventh

Source: GRE test items selected from GRE General Test, Edition GR87-5, Educational Testing Service, (1987). Reprinted by permission of Educational Testing Service.

Disclaimer: Permission to reprint GRE materials does not constitute review or endorsement by Educational Testing Service of this publication as a whole or of any other testing information it may contain.

Exhibit 6.4. Items Assessing
Analytical Reasoning from Course Examinations

Philosophy

The following problem takes place in the Forest of Forgetfulness. The Lion lies on Mondays, Tuesdays, and Wednesdays and tells the truth on the other days of the week. The Unicorn lies on Thursdays, Fridays, and Saturdays and tells the truth the other days. One day Alice met the two in the forest. The Lion said, "I lied yesterday." The Unicorn said, "I lied the day before yesterday or I will tell the truth tomorrow."

Can it be determined what day of the week it is? If so, what day?

Engineering

Given the lottery, we know the following regarding John, Jim, and Larry.

1. John has a certain equivalent of $980 for the lottery.
2. Jim is risk-neutral and has a certain equivalent of $100 for the lottery.
3. Larry has a certain equivalent of $80 for the lottery.

Which of the following is true?

a. John is risk seeking; Larry is more risk seeking than John.
b. John, Jim, and Larry are risk-neutral.
c. John is risk-averse; Larry is more risk-average than John.
d. John is risk seeking but Larry is risk-averse.

Implications for Academic Advising

The faculty in our study were asked which courses they would recommend to students who wanted to improve their abilities in reading comprehension and analytical reasoning. In general, these faculty did not have a consistent knowledge base for making such decisions. When advising, they drew on their own experiences (usually at another college or university), bulletins from the institution at which they currently taught, and word-of-mouth recommendations of courses by other faculty or students.

These faculty generally thought that courses in the disciplines and fields of mathematics, logic, computer science, engineering, philosophy, and biology would help students improve their abilities in analytical reasoning. Some faculty recommended these general areas. Only a few faculty identified or recommended specific courses in their own disciplines. Overall, the faculty were less knowledgeable in recommending courses outside of their own respective disciplines. However, through the CCAM, we found that other courses such as economics, history, psychology, political science, advertising, accounting, and statistics were associated with student improvement in analytical reasoning as well (see Exhibit 6.5).

Faculty generally thought that coursework in the fields of English and literature, as well as writing courses, helped students improve reading comprehension. However, other courses in music, mathematics, French,

Exhibit 6.5. Sample of Courses Associated with Student Improvement in Analytical Reasoning

Course and Number		Course Title
Acct	105	Principles of Accounting I
Chem	31	Chemical Principles
Chem	33	Structure and Reactivity
Econ	1	Elementary Economics
Econ	51	Economics Analysis I
Econ	165	International Economics
Ge	60	Engineering Economics
Hist	1	Europe: Antiquity, Middle Ages, and Renaissance
Hist	2	Europe from Wars of Religion to the Nation State
Hist	3	Europe: 1815 to Present
Math	20	Calculus
Pol Sci	1	Major Issues in American Public Policy
Physics	21	Mechanics and Heat
Psych	106	Cognitive Psychology
Psych	111	Developmental Psychology
Stat	60	Introduction to Statistical Methods I

Exhibit 6.6. Sample of Courses Associated with Student Improvement in Reading Comprehension

Course and Number		Course Title
Fin	203	Principles of Finance
French	2	Elementary French
French	3	Intermediate French
French	4	Intermediate French
Hist	11	Fundamentals of Western Thought
Hist	120	Ireland: Culture & Conflict
HRM	306	Organizational Behavior
Math	105	Math for Decision Making
Mrkt	323	Consumer Behavior
Mu AM	202	Applied Music Major: Instrument
Mu Ed	163	Music in London
Phil	151	Reasoning I
Phys Ed	334	Physiology
Psych	49	Fundamentals of Psychology
TV-R	232	Public Relations
TV-R	241	Advertising

finance, history, psychology, and marketing were also associated with student improvement in reading comprehension (see Exhibit 6.6).

There were many different types of courses and disciplines associated with improvement in student learning. Faculty were tentative inmending general traditional subject areas. When faculty viewed direct recomlinkages of their own discipline with a certain area, they were comfortable in suggesting specific courses in their own disciplines.

Faculty who taught courses associated with improvements in student learning usually clearly stated their course objectives and goals in their syllabi. These objectives represented a mixture of content learning (the subject matter) and cognitive abilities (that is, analytical reasoning and reading comprehension). In this chapter, I have reviewed how faculty sought to develop cognitive abilities that frequently cut across numerous fields or disciplines. The clear objectives that these faculty developed and defined subsequently guided the course examinations that they administered to students. These examinations contained items that assessed student cognitive abilities in reading comprehension and analytical reasoning. These faculty linked the learning that they expected from students, as outlined in the syllabi, to the outcomes assessed on course examinations.

Conclusion

American higher education needs improved student performance, stronger academic direction, and higher standards. Students enter college with a wide variety of backgrounds, life experiences, aptitudes, and educational achievements. The curriculum sequence that is most motivating and is most appropriate to students' educational abilities varies greatly from student to student. College and university faculty that have assessment information can better identify those sets and sequences of courses that are most appropriate for students of a given ability level or with particular interests. With these assessment data, faculty can make stronger substantive links between what students study in college and what they learn.

In the study reported here, faculty who taught specific courses associated with gains in student learning were able to identify how they sought to teach these abilities and how they were assessed. The faculty perceptions generally corroborated the results from the CCAM and they augmented our understanding of how faculty assess student learning in their own courses and the relationships between individual courses and improvements in student learning.

The conventional wisdom that only English classes develop reading comprehension or that only philosophy courses develop analytical reasoning abilities was not confirmed. The groups of courses derived from the CCAM and the faculty interviews suggest that traditional notions about the role of general abilities such as reading comprehension in relation to the structure of knowledge are incomplete. These abilities cut across many fields in both general education and discipline-related courses. Many academic programs or majors have their own philosophy courses, their own statistics courses, their own history courses, and their own methodology courses. Thus, the curriculum is a complex set of interrelated parts that together impact on student learning.

Given the hundreds or thousands of courses in the undergraduate curriculum and given that each course is often designed to produce a distinct contribution to student learning, it is difficult for an individual faculty member to provide timely and accurate advisement to students. Despite these complexities, faculty have yet to develop a solid foundation for offering their advice. When students need to choose among many courses to fulfill specific requirements in general education, faculty members' recollections of their own undergraduate experiences, stereotypical ideas about broad subject areas, or recommendations based on rumors and informal comments passed among students or colleagues do not constitute a sound basis for the construction of an education program. If the CCAM is used for several years, it can isolate consistent groups of courses associated with gains in student learning. With this information, a college or university can develop a stronger, well-informed system of student advisement. For example, courses that consistently enhance low-ability students' learning over time can be identified. Then faculty can advise these students about which courses are most appropriate in order to maximize their learning experiences.

Using data from interviews with faculty who teach courses that are clearly associated with student improvement in specific cognitive abilities, we can begin to develop better insights into how faculty impart skills to their students. Most of the best teachers are still trying to improve their own courses. Through systematic analysis and assessment of coursework patterns, we can acquire better information to help faculty make these improvements in student learning, advisement, and teaching.

References

Astin, A. W. *Assessment for Excellence: The Philosophy and Practice of Assessment and Evaluation in Higher Education.* New York: Macmillan, 1991.

Eaton, J. S. *The Unfinished Agenda: Higher Education and the 1980s.* New York: Macmillan, 1991.

Educational Testing Service. *GRE General Test, Edition GR87-5.* Princeton, N.J.: Educational Testing Service, 1988.

ELIZABETH A. JONES is a research associate at Pennsylvania State University, University Park, where she directs a Fund for the Improvement of Postsecondary Education project that is designed to help the university develop an innovative assessment program for general education. She is also associate editor of the Journal of General Education.

When asked about their perceptions of general education,
undergraduate students reveal their lack of understanding, clarity,
and purpose relative to their general education courses.

General Education: The Insiders' View

Susan B. Twombly

General education as a curriculum form characteristic of U.S. colleges and universities has a long and venerable history. As the ideal core of undergraduate education in the United States since the once homogeneous liberal education gave way to a variety of curriculum options, general education has periodically undergone renewal and reform (Levine, 1986). These efforts are characterized by lofty goals of almost mythical proportions and are imbued with many other trappings of long-held traditions. Prominent faculty members-scholars and researchers of higher education have repeatedly recorded their attempts to define their philosophies of general education, their prescriptions for improved general education, and their observations of unique reforms. This constant attention to general education rests largely on the belief that a general education, in all of its definitions and forms, results in a broadly (read, highly) educated person, whereas a professionally oriented undergraduate education produces a narrowly (read, less) educated individual.

The debate is sometimes rancorous, with general education and professional education often viewed as mutually exclusive. In the absence of actual data to support contentions that one form of general education is better than any other or that generally educated individuals are more intelligent or better citizens than those who have a professional undergraduate preparation, efforts to reform general education find their bases in the commitments, experiences, and personal beliefs of faculty. Furthermore, the focus of most reform efforts is on reaching consensus and, often, compromise on broad, lofty, and ambiguous goals and on an overall package of requirements and courses that students must take. Karen Spear (1989), as vice president and president-elect of the Association of General and Liberal Studies, suggested that general education reform has become a ritualistic activity for faculty that has little meaning in terms of actual education outcomes.

As a ritualistic activity, general education reform efforts are more concerned about the nature of knowledge than with the learning outcomes of day-to-day classroom life. Much curriculum reform treats students as an abstraction and reveals more about the faculty than about student learning (Toombs and Tierney, 1991). Reform efforts stop short of examining actual classroom practice and so ignore how lofty goals of general education programs are translated into actual classroom practice by faculty. This is a crucial oversight. As Gaff (1991, p. 178) has observed: "Curriculum reform does not lead in a straight line to student learning and development. . . . Curriculum change typically starts with agreement on educational goals, about the qualities desired for students. Next, that vision must be incorporated into a curriculum structure and a set of graduation requirements to cultivate those qualities. Then both the purposes and the curriculum need to be understood and affirmed by individual faculty members in their own instructional roles. Next, professors must review and possibly revise their courses to assure that they contribute in the desired ways to the education of students." Despite the common sense nature of Gaff's observation, few colleges follow through on all of these steps. A breakdown seems to occur after intellectual vision is translated into a set of graduation requirements. Most institutions assume that once this set of requirements receives official approval, individual faculty will understand, embrace, and enact the vision through the courses that they teach. In formulating curriculum revision, few institutions seriously consider students' experiences with the curriculum.

In this chapter, I draw on recent research that focused on the perceptions of curriculum "insiders"—students, faculty who teach general education courses, and administrators—to illuminate necessary strategies for curriculum improvement. I look, first, at the meaning that students give to general education, their attitudes toward general education, and their observations about teaching in general education courses. Then I report tentative findings from an exploratory study of faculty enactment of general education goals in the classroom. Finally, I offer recommendations for effective curriculum planning.

Students' Perceptions of General Education

Richard Light, director of the Harvard Assessment Seminars, emphasized the importance of listening to what students have to say about their learning experiences: "Students have thought a lot about what works well for them. We can learn much from their insights. Often their insights are far more helpful, and more subtle, than a vague 'common wisdom' about how faculty members can help students to make good decisions at college" (1992, p. 6). What can faculty and administrators learn from students? The available literature that specifically addresses students' perceptions of general education is meager but suggests the following:

General Education Is Synonymous With Well Rounded. Students almost universally define general education as exposure to a wide range of subjects, some of which they would not study if not required. Students value a broad general education, particularly if that general education relates to their professional goals and self-knowledge (Gaff and Davis, 1981; Twombly, in press). Specifically, they place high value on effective communication skills, cognitive or thinking skills, and interpersonal skills (Newmann, 1987; Gaff and Davis, 1981; Twombly, 1992). General knowledge, students believe, is essential to their efforts to become well-rounded people, a quality that is necessary for effective communication with others (Twombly, 1992). This notion of a well-rounded education was, in fact, the goal of general education most commonly reported by students in a variety of majors at a major research university (Twombly, 1992). The clearer the vision that students, regardless of major, seem to have of their future professions, and of all that these professionals entail, the more the students are able to articulate their understanding of general education and the value that they place on it. In fact, in the absence of clearly defined career goals, liberal arts students seemed to struggle with the question of how general education courses are or are not useful to them. Few viewed general education as having any intrinsic value other than to make them well rounded.

General Education Serves Instrumental and Personal Development Purposes. Students report that general education courses provide experience for the real world by enabling them to establish their academic confidence and to build study habits. General education also provides an opportunity for students to choose majors, a safety net if their intended majors do not work out, and an opportunity, particularly for those in professional programs, to meet other students from different majors (Twombly, in press). To a much lesser extent, general education is perceived to contribute to personal development goals such as obtaining a better understanding of self. Certain courses, such as general psychology, that deal with stress and other related topics important to students, are specifically identified as contributing to personal development.

Intended Career Seems to Have the Most Significant Influence on Students' Understanding of the Meaning and Importance of General Education. Like it or not, much evidence points to intended careers as the major influences on students' understanding of and attitudes toward general education (Gaff and Davis, 1981; Johnston and others, 1991; Twombly, in press). Students seem to formulate their conceptions of general education in relation to their understanding of the requirements of their intended professions. For example, some engineering students envision a relatively short career as entry-level engineers and much longer careers as managers-engineers. In this case, students recognize the value of communication skills, both written and spoken, and the ability to relate to people. Nurses also understand that general education courses such as mathematics and ethics are specifically related to their professional education and to their future careers as nurses. In short, as Johnston and others (1991, p. 184) have observed, "Most students come to college to prepare for a career," and they identify course requirements as either useful or useless in relation to their career goals.

Other influences pale in comparison. A variety of people, especially family members, influence students' understanding of the purposes of general education, but faculty members and advisers occupy a noticeably nonprominent position on this list. In fact, some students say that most faculty and advisers do not want to talk about the purposes of general education (Twombly, in press). When asked why students have to take general education courses, faculty members-advisers most commonly state the goal of making students well rounded. Faculty members do in fact influence students' understanding of general education but not, perhaps, in expected or intended ways. They do so implicitly through their courses: their assignments and examinations, their methods of teaching, the content of their courses, and so on.

Out-of-Class Experiences and Nonacademic Units May Do Little to Support General Education Objectives. Based on an extensive review of the literature, Johnston and others (1991) concluded that out-of-class experiences and nonacademic units on campus, most notably student services, did little to support general education goals. In particular, new student orientation, an opportune and critical time for new students, seems to do little to inform students about the meaning and purpose of general education.

Students Have Modest Expectations of General Education Courses. Students expect an overview or broad general knowledge of subjects, but often they report too much "unnecessary" detail (Johnston and others, 1991; Twombly, in press). They also expect the courses to be interesting through the efforts of the instructors.

Choice of General Education Distribution Courses Is Often Based on a Complex Formula. The formula differs for each student but includes such practical considerations as degree of difficulty, time of day offered, workload expectations balanced with other demands, grade point average, and interest (Becker, Geer, and Hughes, 1968; Mofatt, 1989; Twombly, 1992). Despite idealistic hopes that students might choose general education courses for higher-minded reasons such as intrinsic value of the subjects, students are very pragmatic when it comes to exercising their choices.

Students Study Less for General Education Courses than for Major Courses. Generally speaking, students report less study for general education courses than for courses related to their intended majors. Study strategies for general education mainly involve learning material for a test "and then forgetting it." For students, memorization of facts is the major strategy called for in general education courses. Students are particularly irritated when they have to work harder in their general education courses than in their majors' courses (Twombly, in press). Loss of study time from their majors or points from their grade point averages seems to be a major concern for students.

As much as faculty and parents might implore students to focus on learning and not on grade point average or "the rules for the test," Becker, Geer, and Hughes's (1968) findings seem as valid today as they were when the study was conducted. Much to my disappointment, my personal experiences in teaching four undergraduate semesters of Spanish confirm that most students are so concerned about grades that they really just want to do whatever they have to do to get a certain grade on tests and in the course. Unfortunately, the system of grades and tests feeds this preoccupation. It would be easy for me to conclude that most students care little about actually learning Spanish. Obsession with rules for tests seems almost to be a strategy for removing some of the responsibility from themselves for not doing well. But in the absence of additional research, this would be a simplistic and unfair conclusion. Light (1992) reported that foreign language courses were among the most appreciated at Harvard, and I have to believe that students really do feel a sense of accomplishment when they learn a foreign language.

Teaching in General Education Courses

The issue of study strategies and the influence of teachers on students' perceptions of general education led me to look at what students have to say about teaching in general education courses. Much can be learned about an institution's general education goals by examining not only students' reported perceptions of teaching but also the extent to which a college's general education goals are adopted and implemented by faculty in the classroom. In separate analyses, Johnston and others (1991) and I (Twombly, in press) found that most students, when asked to indicate whether courses accomplished a list of goals traditionally associated with general education, reported that most courses failed to achieve each of the aims listed. The students interviewed in my study laughed or expressed a profound sense of confusion when public statements of general education goals for their academic unit were read to them. These students obviously did not recognize that general education goals were explicitly expressed in their courses.

What kinds of messages about general education do students receive in their courses? Students in a variety of majors at the research university where I conducted my study observed that there was a great deal of redundancy in general education courses (Twombly, 1992). While some students jokingly said that this saved them money, they generally felt that it was a waste of their precious time to use the same book and to cover the same material in two or three different courses. More than anything else, the redundancy seemed to communicate to them that the faculty did not really work together to create a coordinated set of learning experiences. And while the students expected and wanted general knowledge in their general education courses, many observed that they were bombarded by facts at a level of detail that they neither needed nor would remember. Students suggested that they were expected to master some subject or professional knowledge in depth and that it was just not possible to learn too many subjects in any depth. They also seemed to believe in a division of labor. That is, in the workplace or real world, someone else would be an expert in the areas in which they were not proficient.

With respect to the higher-order thinking skills typically associated with general education goals, the picture is discouraging. Students in my study reported that there was an emphasis on memorization and regurgitation of the "right" answers and that attempts at what students thought to be critical thinking were often squelched, especially in English classes (Twombly, in press). In contrast, there was some evidence that science classes better rewarded critical thinking. For these classes, the descriptions of teaching were more in line with our hopes for general education courses. For example, an engineering student said, "I took Econ 140 last semester. I thought it was the best class I've taken. I loved it. . . . I got to think. I also got to do something nonengineering. I got to look at different things in different ways, and my teacher taught me when you read an article about economics in the *Wall Street Journal,* you can tell what's going on. A lot of times what politicians say about unemployment and what they're going to try to do is just a bunch of bull. . . . It really taught you how to think for yourself. It wasn't just a bunch of formulas." Another student credited an art teacher for teaching her a lot about general ideas even though art was not her intended major. Regardless of whether students' negative impressions are valid, these are the perceptions that many students have of their general education courses. It is almost as if the purpose of general education courses is to fill students with facts and that higher-order thinking skills come later.

Another disturbing factor has to do with the role of advising in shaping students' understanding of general education. Students have ambivalent feelings about advising: They often do not want too much but complain when they do not get enough attention. According to students, many advisers sign students' schedules without much questioning, and many are hesitant to discuss the purposes of general education with students. Well-roundedness seems to define advisers' explanations of why students have to take general education courses (Gaff and Davis, 1981; Johnston and others, 1991; Twombly, 1992). Some possible explanations for the above observations of teaching emerge when we look at faculty's understanding of general education and their role in it.

Implementation of General Education Goals

Even though there is little research on how students understand and interpret general education, the existing research points to a gap between the sometimes lofty goals of college catalogues and actual courses. Or, as Gaff (1991) suggests, there is a slippage in the process of translating purposes into curriculum structure and courses. As a first step in designing more effective general education curricula, faculty and administrators must understand and, perhaps more important, care about what happens in this process of translating goals into action. It is, of course, difficult to translate vague goals, such as wisdom, into classroom experiences.

In exploratory research that I recently conducted, the goal was to identify how faculty and administrators responsible for general education at four very different institutions understood and supported general education goals, either through the classroom or through administrative support activities. One study was conducted at a typical suburban community college, for which there was no coordinated set of well-defined goals for general education, and at a comprehensive state university, which had recently revised its general education program. This university has a well-defined set of general education goals spelled out clearly in the university's catalogue. Moreover, there is a committee and an administrator whose responsibility is to monitor the general education program. This administrator indicated that he occasionally meets with faculty to discuss general education goals for their classes. Commitment to general education seems high at this university. At each of these institutions, faculty who teach general education courses were randomly selected from science, social science, and humanities fields to participate in the study. They were asked about the institutions' general education goals, the goals of their courses, and the relationship between the institutions' goals and their course objectives. It is important to note that the faculty interviewed were "regular" faculty as opposed to those heavily involved in curriculum planning. A second study was conducted at a traditional, selective liberal arts college and at one of the nation's distinguished major research universities. This study focused on administrators' understanding of and support for general education.

Although each study was guided by somewhat different research questions, the major purpose of each was to examine how faculty and administrators understand and enact general education goals in the class-room and in the college or university overall. Based on these two studies, observations can be made that provide food for thought for those faculty and administrators who spend their valuable time and efforts reforming the general education curriculum in the name of student learning. Due to the exploratory nature of the studies, the following observations should be viewed as tentative propositions requiring further study.

First and perhaps foremost, if there is any relationship between an institution's general education goals and what is taught in general educa-tion classes, it is purely accidental. That is, when planning courses and setting course objectives, the faculty typically did not refer to their insti-tutions' general education goals. Most did not even know their own institution's general education goals, although they indicated that the goals were listed in the catalogue. Faculty, like students, tend to describe general education in terms of specific course requirements (Tonjes, in progress). Surprising as it may seem, faculty do not articulate general education goals in a very sophisticated manner.

Second, regardless of institutional type or how well defined and articulated the general education goals, faculty generally do not attend to the general education goals of their institution. Even when an institution has a general education committee and an administrator who oversees general education, the general education goals of the university are not primary in the minds of faculty when they plan their general education courses. This observation does not mean that faculty fail to accomplish the institution's general education goals or other important curriculum goals, just that the institution's polished statements of goals do not drive what goes on in the classroom.

Third, despite the fact that some outspoken faculty write eloquently about the meaning and purposes of general education and that institutional statements of general education are often very deep and profound, many faculty define the meaning and purpose of general education in the same way as students: to provide a well-rounded education. Furthermore, faculty tend to articulate the institution's philosophy of general education in terms of graduation requirements. Their own courses are merely pieces in this jigsaw puzzle of graduation requirements, which when completed will equal well-rounded, well-educated individuals. Faculty claim little overt responsibility for integrative general education goals. They do, however, often cite skill-related goals among their course objectives.

If faculty tend not to rely on the institution's stated general education goals in planning their own courses, what do they use as a guide? In the absence of a well-defined set of general education goals, community college faculty seem to plan courses that count toward the general educa-tion requirement with the college's mission and clientele in mind. Often, these faculty speak about the relationship between their disciplinary subjects and the students' real lives. For faculty in a comprehensive university, the disciplines and faculty expertise seem to drive the content of general education courses. Again, this is not to say that faculty do not accomplish very real general education goals in their courses. It is just that their guidance tends to come from the disciplines and their own understanding of the disciplines and what a well-rounded person should know about the disciplines and not from any agreed-on institutional statement of the purposes of general education.

Although faculty may talk frequently with each other about what works and what does not in their classes, seldom do they specifically discuss general education goals and how the courses that they offer individually or collectively support and convey general education goals. This lack of discussion may in part explain the redundancy in course content that students report.

Fourth, administrators have an ambivalent relationship with general education curricula. When deans and other administrators believe that they have made a contribution to curriculum planning, they see it as part of their faculty role. Midlevel managers, often nonfaculty, tend to see themselves and their jobs as crucial to the process of delivering general education. Faculty believe that institutional support and rewards for participation in general education are minimal; however, administrators seem to believe that faculty receive intrinsic rewards from involvement in general education and that external rewards are not necessary.

Faculty, students, and administrators seem to agree that there is little attempt to explain the institution's philosophy for general education to students. This is even true for liberal arts colleges. Most existing efforts rely on outlines of course requirements. Whether it would make a difference in learning outcomes if students understood the intended purposes of general education is not known. Regardless of the exploratory nature of much of the research in this area, there is clearly a huge gap between curriculum planning efforts and implementation in the classroom. The process seems to break down after goals and curriculum structure are agreed on. In the culture of higher education organizations, classroom activities are viewed as largely private matters between faculty and students, which may contribute to this gap between principles and practices.

Recommendations for Effective Curriculum Planning

Given the prominence of general education in U.S. colleges and universities, it is likely that efforts to reform it will continue. The question that faces all institutions is how they can make their time and effort well spent. Gaff (1991), among others, has cited the importance of faculty development to sincere efforts to improve general education programs. Clearly, faculty development is crucial, but I argue here that in order to be effective, faculty development must recognize what is important to faculty and take into account what happens in the classroom. To facilitate this effort, students' perceptions and experiences must be taken into account. Based on the findings of the research to date, some practical recommendations for curriculum planning can be made.

First, much can be learned about the real curriculum—the one that is delivered in the classroom—by asking students about their perceptions of teaching and learning in the classroom. Efforts should be made regularly to solicit student feedback on these issues. Regardless of faculty intentions, if students understand them differently, their interpretations constitute an important reality that cannot be ignored. Most institutions have some systematic means to formally evaluate teaching. It would be relatively simple to add a few questions to the evaluation form that ask students about course goals and general education outcomes. Interviews with students in diverse majors can add an important dimension to survey data. This kind of systematic data collection over a wide range of courses and over a number of years is essential.

Second, faculty development and curriculum-planning efforts in support of general education must recognize the importance that students place on the relationship of general education to their future careers and the ties that faculty have to disciplines. Rather than pit general education against professional education or view general education as the one opportunity that faculty have to broaden students' horizons, it may be more productive to link general and professional education together. This is not a new idea. The classical liberal arts curriculum that characterized higher education in the eighteenth and nineteenth centuries was highly professional. Recent proponents of this linkage (Sagan, 1979; Stark, Lowther, and Hagerty, 1986; Marsh, 1988) have argued not only that the purposes of liberal and professional education are similar but also that general education goals might be better achieved in relation to professional education. The few who have dared to be vocal in their support of this view seem to be shouting in the wind, however. The importance that students place on careers seems unlikely to change in the near future, and general education might be more effectively accomplished by recognizing and building on this fact.

The other side of this coin is that for faculty, the disciplines provide the basis for their approach to general education courses. Faculty development efforts might better be directed at enhancing understanding of the relationship of the disciplines to general knowledge rather than merely at strengthening interdisciplinary ties. For most faculty, their courses seem to be just pieces in the jigsaw puzzle of a college education. Individually, they determine how much of the disciplines students need to know. And they engage in little discussion of how one piece fits together with other courses or disciplines to create the whole. Faculty do, however, pay attention to the cutting-edge developments in their disciplines, and these are, it seems, the most effective targets of faculty development efforts for general education. Professional disciplinary associations provide a good starting point.

Third, once a curriculum is adopted and implemented, faculty spend little time talking with each other about general education goals and how their courses accomplish those goals. Even though an institution often has publicly stated goals for general education, what goes on in the individual courses that make up general education is viewed as private and off-limits. Faculty development efforts should not assume that curriculum goals are adopted by faculty and implemented in the classroom. If curriculum goals are important, an effort needs to be made to make faculty and students aware of them and to keep them in the foreground of faculty in particular. In fact, one might argue that the biggest fault of curriculum planners is that the curriculum is seldom implemented as designed, if at all. I visited one four-year liberal arts college in the process of implementing a new core curriculum. They were in the midst of a two-day session in which the faculty responsible for the core courses were sharing their individual course objectives and content. This exchange was an eye-opening experience for most of them and an extremely important step toward making their core effective. If nothing else, such an approach eliminates or minimizes redundancy for students. The student outcomes assessment movement has focused attention on this area, but greater attention needs to be paid to implementation issues.

Fourth, perhaps too much emphasis is placed on a single set of courses or experiences to accomplish lofty general education goals. As described by Miller (1988, p. 5), general education is a product of a specific set of specific courses:

> [General education is] a comprehensive, self-consciously developed and maintained program that develops in individual students the attitudes of inquiry; the skills of problem solving; the individual and community values associated with a democratic society; and the knowledge needed to apply these attitudes, skills and values so that the students may maintain the learning process over a lifetime and function as self-fulfilled individuals and full participants in a society committed to change through democratic processes. As such, it is marked by its comprehensive scope, by its emphasis on specific and real problems and issues of immediate concern to students and society, by its concern with the needs of the future, and by the application of democratic principles in the methods and procedures as well as the goals of education.

This statement clearly reflects an ideal rather than common practice; and even if it were an accurate description, it is unreasonable to expect a single set of courses to accomplish such lofty goals. Students tend not to draw the distinctions among curriculum components that scholars and faculty draw, and they are probably correct in viewing general education requirements as one piece in their total educational experience, which includes nonacademic aspects of colleges and universities as well.

Like Johnston and others (1991), my position is that general education goals cannot be accomplished unless out-of-class experiences and services are actively embraced within an institution's intellectual education goals and engaged in the education of students. At one college that I visited, the theme or overriding philosophy of the new core curriculum was freedom and responsibility. During my visit, I asked if student affairs had been involved in discussions to help the college achieve its objectives. It seems almost impossible for general education goals such as these to be accomplished without the support of the entire institution. It also is unlikely that one set of core courses can accomplish all of the goals set for this core curriculum. The boundaries of where general education begins and ends and where professional or the depth portion of education begins and ends are not clear. It is perhaps futile to spend inordinate amounts of time revising only one minor (in the minds of most students) portion of the academic experience without attending to the complete experience. Surely, some faculty development efforts need to be directed toward faculty understanding and valuing of the relevance of the total educational experience in achieving general education objectives. Administrators also need to see a valid role for themselves in the true academic function of the institution, and they need to be willing and able to support in-class objectives with out-of-class activities and experiences.

Finally, colleges and universities can do a much better job of explaining the purposes of education to students. There is no evidence that explanations of general education goals to students improve general education outcomes. However, in the absence of such explanations, students' only recourse in their efforts to understand the purposes of their educational experience is to rely on various external forces and the messages that they receive in their classes. These messages, it would appear, are not totally satisfactory. One relatively easy way to explain general education goals might be in the context of writing classes. It is clear that faculty do not make a special effort to integrate curriculum experiences for students. So if we expect students to detect the relationships among the things that they learn, then we must help them to make the desired connections by making connections with other bodies of knowledge. Finally, if they accomplish nothing else, efforts to explain the purposes of education to students would reinforce the importance of general education.

In this chapter, I have reviewed the findings of several recent studies to emphasize that curriculum-planning efforts can be greatly improved by listening to students' impressions of general education and by focusing attention on how general education goals are enacted by faculty in the classroom. Until such steps are taken, current and future efforts to reform general education are not likely to be any more successful than were their many predecessors.

References

Becker, H., Geer, B., and Hughes, E. *Making the Grade: The Academic Side of College Life*. New York: Wiley, 1968.

Gaff, J. G. *New Life for the College Curriculum: Assessing Achievements and Furthering Progress in the Reform of General Education*. San Francisco: Jossey-Bass, 1991.

Gaff, J. G., and Davis, M. "Student Views of General Education." *Liberal Education*, 1981, 67 (2), 112–123.

Johnston, J., Jr., and others. "The Demand Side of General Education: Attending to Student Attitudes and Understandings." *Journal of General Education*, 1991, 40, 180–200.

Levine, D. *The American College and the Culture of Aspiration, 1915–1940*. Ithaca, N.Y.: Cornell University Press, 1986.

Light, R. *The Harvard Assessment Seminars: Second Report*. Cambridge, Mass.: Harvard University Press, 1992.

Marsh, P. *Contesting the Boundaries of Liberal and Professional Education*. Syracuse, N.Y.: Syracuse University Press, 1988.

Miller, G. E. *The Meaning of General Education: The Emergence of a Paradigm*. New York: Teachers College Press, 1988.

Moffat, M. *Coming of Age in New Jersey*. New Brunswick: Rutgers University Press, 1989.

Newmann, L. "Student Perspectives and Curricular Evaluation." Paper presented at the annual meeting of the American Association of Higher Education, Washington, D.C., 1987.

Sagen, B. H. "Career, Competencies, and Liberal Education." *Liberal Education*, 1979, 65, 150–166.

Spear, K. "Sources of Strain in Liberal Education." *Review of Higher Education*, 1989, 12, 389–401.

Stark, J., Lowther, M., and Hagerty, B. *Responsive Professional Education*. ASHE-ERIC Higher Education Reports, no. 3. Washington, D.C.: Association for the Study of Higher Education, 1986.

Tonjes, N. "General Education and Institutional Culture: A Case Study Approach." Unpublished doctoral dissertation, University of Kansas, forthcoming.

Toombs, W., and Tierney, W. G. *Meeting the Mandate: Renewing the College and Departmental Curriculum*. ASHE/ERIC Higher Education Report No. 6. Washington, D.C.: Association for the Study of Higher Education, 1991.

Twombly, S. B. "Students' Perspectives on General Education in a Research University: An Exploratory Study." *Journal of General Education*, 1992, 41, 238–272.

SUSAN B. TWOMBLY is associate professor of higher education at the University of Kansas, Lawrence. Her interests include administrative labor markets in higher education, community colleges, and gender issues.

INDEX

Ordering Information

New Directions for Higher Education is a series of paperback books that provides timely information and authoritative advice about major issues and administrative problems confronting every institution. Books in the series are published quarterly in spring, summer, fall, and winter and are available for purchase by subscription as well as by single copy.

Subscriptions for 1992 cost $45.00 for individuals (a savings of 20 percent over single-copy prices) and $60.00 for institutions, agencies, and libraries. Please do not send institutional checks for personal subscriptions. Standing orders are accepted.

Single copies cost $14.95 when payment accompanies order. (California, New Jersey, New York, and Washington, D.C., residents please include appropriate sales tax.) Billed orders will be charged postage and handling.

Discounts for quantity orders are available. Please write to the address below for information.

All orders must include either the name of an individual or an official purchase order number. Please submit your order as follows:
    Subscriptions: specify series and year subscription is to begin
    Single copies: include individual title code (such as HE1)

Mail all orders to:
    Jossey-Bass Publishers
    350 Sansome Street
    San Francisco, California 94104

OTHER TITLES AVAILABLE IN THE
NEW DIRECTIONS FOR HIGHER EDUCATION SERIES
Martin Kramer, Editor-in-Chief